VINTAGE CAR ANNUAL

EDITED by MIKE WORTHINGTON-WILLIAMS

PUBLISHED BY
MARSHALL HARRIS & BALDWIN LTD
17 AIR STREET LONDON W1

INTRODUCING OURSELVES

WAY back in 1962 a small group calling themselves North London Artists gathered together to produce, as a labour of love, a different kind of magazine for early vehicle enthusiasts. Called *VINTAGE COMMERCIAL*, it was an instant success and a few months later was joined by a sister publication, *OLD MOTOR*, which was designed to cater for those more interested in cars and motorcycles. Both titles were combined in July 1963 and later shortened to *OLD MOTOR* to give coverage to the whole spectrum of early vehicle activity and interest with pre-1960 cars, commercials, steam vehicles and motorcycles all receiving equal treatment.

During sixteen years of successful publication, *OLD MOTOR* built up a unique library of early photographs and gradually assembled a team of writers, all of whom were leaders in their respective fields. They were joined in 1964 by Mike Worthington-Williams, the editor of this annual, who has contributed regularly to the pages of *OLD MOTOR* whilst also editing *VETERAN CAR* magazine for the Veteran Car Club of Great Britain, helping to set up the international Society of Automotive Historians, sitting on the Veteran Car Club Dating Committee, and writing books and articles for many of our contemporaries. He is also head of Sotheby's vintage vehicle department and organises and catalogues all their early vehicle sales.

We live in an age of specialisation, however, and increasingly, as the early vehicle hobby has progressed over the years, enthusiasts have tended to concentrate upon those vehicles which

interest them most, and as costs have risen, it has become more and more difficult to provide a multi-interest magazine giving the kind of in-depth coverage for which *OLD MOTOR* became well known, which would appeal to those whose main interest lay in, perhaps, cars only - or lorries, or buses.

The answer, clearly, was to change direction. The photographic library and the writing team provided the scope for a series of *KALEIDO-SCOPE* books, and so far titles published include *FARM TRAC-TORS, MOTORCYCLES and LORRIES*, and specialist titles on steam wagons, AC Cars, Leo Villa's life with the Campbells, Richard Shuttleworth, Shelvoke & Drewry and many others are in course of preparation. So successful have these books been that we shall also be producing Vintage Annuals on a variety of particular subjects, including this one on Cars, and embracing others on Lorries, Buses and Motorcycling with, we hope, Farm Tractors and Machinery to follow as well.

Since most publishers prefer to concentrate on the more lucrative 'mass market' subjects, we feel that with both *KALEIDOSCOPES* and Annuals, we will be continuing to give coverage on both popular and offbeat subjects, but in a more specialised and detailed way, as we did in the pages of *OLD MOTOR* (which now continues under new ownership as a popular monthly). Sixteen years of preserving and writing about early vehicles has taught us what an important and discriminating section of the early vehicle movement wants.

The publishing house of Marshall, Harris and Baldwin Ltd, under whose imprint the books are appearing, therefore is new in name only. The experience and the quality is the same as that which readers have come to expect, and the same team as before is still involved.

The study of automobiles and motoring history, with its colourful manufacturing and racing personalities, is probably the fastest growing hobby since the war and we on the Vintage Car Annual team have been privileged to have been part of it and to have contributed to it by presenting those facts which frequently were unobtainable elsewhere. When we became involved all those years ago, automobile history was scarcely considered a serious subject for scholars and historians alike, but we set out to make it so and we hope that those of you who read and enjoy this unique selection of previously unpublished articles and photographs will agree that we have succeeded in our aim.

History need not be dry as dust, and by combining a sense of perspective with technical and human background, we can portray the events, struggles and endeavours of yesteryear more accurately for what they are - the day-to-day hopes, fears and amusing incidents of today's motorists and motor industry, recalled in years to come.

From only one club - The Veteran Car Club of Great Britain - in 1930, the old car preservation movement has grown so that today scarcely a single country exists which does not boast its own club and band of enthusiasts. We have watched this growth - growing pains included - with interest and pleasure, and participated in it both practically and editorially. We feel that our Vintage Car Annuals and *KALEIDOSCOPE* books are the best way in which we can illustrate our love of the subject and share it with our transport friends all over the world.

We hope that you will enjoy this, the first of the Car Annuals, and that you will buy future editions as they appear each year. Let us know what you think of it and remember, we are always pleased to hear from you with your latest vehicle and archive discoveries and news of your restorations. Whilst we cannot promise to reply individually to every letter we receive, we find all your comments of interest and they will be a great help to us when we are planning future issues, and compiling letters and news columns for the 1980 issue.

POTTED PALMS & DOUBLE SIXES

**With rationalisation triumphant and many of today's marques masquerading
separate identities behind badge engineering, lovers of individuality tend to find
motor shows of the seventies - and, indeed, most of our roads - rather arid affairs.
It was not always so, and in this cameo of the twenties CLIFFORD S PENNY recalls
the days when schoolboys were welcome at Olympia and White City,
and kerbside car identification was one of the keenest followed hobbies.**

I attended my first Olympia Motor Show in 1926, having just achieved the status of a teenager. The main purpose of my visit was to scrutinise the radiator badges of the more uncommon makes, so that I could readily identify them if encountered on the road.

The car that created the most interest at this Show was the Daimler Double Six, the first British twelve cylinder car to be offered to the public. At this time it was the only twelve cylinder car in production in the world, for earlier 'twelves', such as the Packard Twin Six, had been dropped from their manufacturers' programmes by 1926. The Double Six was a massive car of great dignity, and gathered a large and respectful crowd

The potted palms of Olympia. The dogtooth pattern 'tiled' linoleum, tasseled rope barriers and elaborately decorative proscenia proclaimed the individuality of the myriad marques hopefully displayed there. The whole impression of a rather grand circus slightly frayed round the edges is highlighted by the scuffed barriers and the oil patches from incontinent sumps in the foreground - rather like the inevitable horse droppings in any street scene of the pre-First War period.

The sheer grandeur and unashamed opulence of these factory bodied Daimler Double Six 50hp landaulettes would have been bound to earn the admiration of any callow youth in 1927/8, although a few years later such luxury would only have been tolerated for royalty. The pennant fluttering from the radiator cap of the right hand car and the numbered sticker on the windscreen might denote just that.

around it. However, en route to the Daimler stand I had had my first sight of an Isotta Fraschini, and to me this seemed the most beautiful machine I had ever seen in my life. Its elegance and panache still lingers in my memory.

I next attended the 1928 Show, travelling there in a 1912 Rover two seater, which to me seemed incredibly ancient. I recall that a row of switches ran the length of the dashboard, each lamp having its individual switch. The owner would leave the car parked in unfrequented side streets for hours on end, hoping that it would be stolen, thus enabling him to make a claim on his insurance company!

I visited the last vintage Motor Show in 1930, when such wonderful cars as the 8 litre Bentley, the Grosser Mercedes and the V16 Cadillac made their London debut. I have not attended a London Motor Show since that golden year.

One of the joys of the Show for me

was the mass of literature on display to allure prospective purchasers. On the Trojan stand a large orange coloured carrier bag was available, *gratis*, in which to stow catalogues and brochures. The cheaper cars seemed to generate the most in the way of publicity material, the luxury auto-mobiles providing little or nothing in this respect. I was never able to obtain anything in print about the Rolls-Royce, although I once discovered a pile of photographs on the Hispano Suiza stand, one of which found its way into my Trojan bag. Another marked difference in sales technique between the popular and luxury cars was that, while the salesmen on such stands as Morris and Austin cordially invited all and sundry to sample the comfort of the seat cushions, such hospitality was sadly lacking on the stands selling expensive cars, the doors of these exclusive carriages being kept securely locked.

I staggered home with sufficient reading matter to occupy me for a week. Young noses are keen, and I remember that the paper used for American catalogues had a distinctive odour about it. Had I kept all this literature it would by now have acquired quite a useful pecuniary value, not forgetting the pleasure to be obtained by browsing through it again. The same remarks apply to the vintage era issues of *The Autocar* and

The Motor, which were carefully filed by me until the loft in our North London home could no longer contain them, whereupon they were consigned to the dustbin. I wonder if the dustmen realised that he was handling material which would later turn into gold.

In retrospect, I am amazed at the equanimity with which the salesmen regarded the numerous schoolboys swarming over the stands at Olympia. However, there may have been a sound commercial reason for this tolerance, for I recall an affable salesman saying to me, as I was helping myself to a generous fistful of literature, 'I expect the pater will be along later'.

Mention of the Trojan bag reminds me that this car was very popular with the clergy - it was probably the only make ever to be advertised in the *Church Times*. Some garages were so bemused by its mechanical complexity that they put up a defiant notice reading 'No Trojans'. In standard form the Trojan was fitted with solid tyres, although pneumatics were available as an optional extra, where-upon travel in the car became, to quote the manufacturers, 'sheer luxury'. The fear that solid tyred models might get wedged in tramlines was probably groundless, although wags of the day conjured up visions of

the Trojan ending its journey in the tramway depôt.

Memories of vintage Motor Shows include the enormous crowds, nowhere to take the weight off one's feet, long queues for refreshments and a stifling atmosphere. Such discomforts were as nothing compared with the privilege of being able to see the cream of the world's automobile industry under one roof. It must be conceded, though, that there were one or two notable absentees - no Lincoln, Maybach or Pierce-Arrow appeared at Olympia during the vintage era.

The World's Land Speed Record attracted great interest during the nineteen twenties, and I remember the horror I felt on reading of the death of J G Parry Thomas while driving *Babs* at Pendine in 1927. In 1923 I was, for a short time, a patient in The Hospital for Sick Children in Great Ormond Street, London. During my stay there a regular visitor to the ward was a quiet, unassuming man who took obvious pleasure in chatting to the youngsters. Much later, I learned that this man was none other than Parry Thomas, who had endowed a cot at

The car that 'towered above all the rest of the field'. The 1925 14/40 Sunbeam which went to the breakers for £5 in 1939 when, with war threatening, you couldn't give such cars away. It is remembered with affection.

the hospital. After his tragic death, *The Autocar* raised a subscription to endow the cot for posterity as a fitting memorial to him. It is known as the Babs Cot.

Captain Malcolm Campbell's success with the Napier-Campbell at Daytona in 1928 prompted me to write to him suggesting various improvements to the streamlining of his car. This was confounded cheek on my part for, needless to say, I was not handicapped by any knowledge of the subject. However, in due course I received a reply from this national hero giving reasons why my 'improvements' were not feasible. He did say, nevertheless, that the enclosing of the wheels, as was done with Lockhart's

Stutz, another contender for the Land Speed Record, might have had some merit.

In 1926 my family spent a holiday at Hove and during our stay a local newspaper covered a court case involving a motorist summonsed for 'driving at a speed dangerous to the public' along the sea front at Brighton. The headlines read 'Eighty

Seat of Government. Clifford Penny's youthful enthusiasm for the Grosser Mercedes would have been unclouded by Nazi associations when this 1931 770K 1st series appeared. Fitted with the Maybach Schnellgang overdrive [with controls on the steering wheel boss] the interior was strictly functional despite the luxury, and the gear and brake levers owe more to truck design than to *haute couture*.

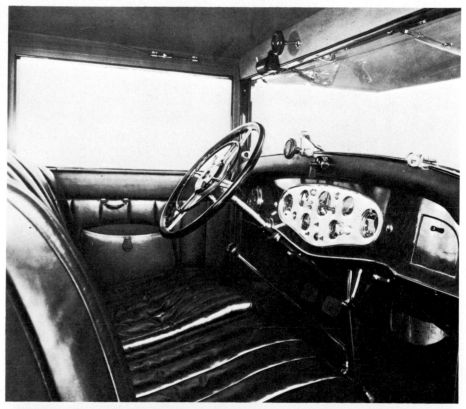

The Daimler stand at Olympia in 1927. Behind the pillar the thin strip dividing the radiator denotes a Double Six 50 - the smaller 30 introduced at the Show and sharing the dimensions of the 16/55 Six, is behind it. In the foreground is a six cylinder 25/85 landaulette.

Miles an Hour on King's Road - "Flying Scotsman" Driver Fined'. Giving evidence, a police officer said that he estimated the car's speed at between 35 and 40 mph. However, the driver told the magistrates, with commendable honesty, that when he was passing the Hotel Metropole his speed might have been 80 mph. The accused was a Major Ian Grant, an engineer home on leave from India, who was the only volunteer to drive *The Flying Scotsman* during the General Strike of 1926. The newspaper report stated that he was at the wheel of a 'powerful Sunbeam motor car' - no doubt a 3 litre twin ohc model.

The Galloping Major was fined £4 with £1 costs; his licence was not endorsed. Such a performance in King's Road would appear to have qualified him for participation in the Brighton Speed Trials held in the nearby Madeira Drive!

At Northaw in Hertfordshire, a large estate was owned by an aunt of Lieutenant Commander Glen Kidston, the well-known racing motorist and 'Bentley Boy'. Living at Potters Bar, I used to see the Commander at the wheel of a white Hispano Suiza on his way to visit this relative. His driving could be justifiably described as dashing, and on one occasion a leading local resident had to move very quickly in order to escape annihilation.

At the age of thirteen I had a letter published in *The Motor*, much to my surprise and delight. A year or two later I became somewhat exasperated by constant letters to the motoring press from Mr S F Edge, extolling the merits of the AC car. Not having the courage to pen a letter of protest over my own signature, I persuaded my twin brother to write to the Editor of the magazine concerned, expressing surprise that he permitted his correspondence columns to be used by Mr Edge for advertising purposes. The letter duly appeared in print and, in a footnote to it, the Editor said that it was only in exceptional circumstances that letters from manufacturers were published.

When I became old enough to hold a driving licence, the cars at my disposal were not of the same standing as the Isotta Fraschini or the Daimler Double Six. It was the popular cars of the day, such as the Austin Seven, Morris Cowley and Singer Junior which provided me with much enjoyable motoring. However, one car owned by the family is still remembered with great affection - a 14/40hp Sunbeam drophead coupé of 1925 vintage. It was purchased around 1936 for £30 (its original cost was nearly £700) and went to the breaker's yard at the outbreak of the Second World War for the sum of £5. The car could be easily picked out in a crowded car park, for it towered above the rest of the field. Slamming the doors produced the same satisfactory sound as that made by the door of a first class railway carriage. I am told that if the car had survived to the present day its value would be in excess of £5000.

These random reminiscences may revive memories for some who were fortunate enough to be young at a time when cars and coachwork were at such an exciting period of development and, aesthetically speaking, at their zenith.

ROBBINS
OF PUTNEY

**The period 1898-1979 encompasses virtually the whole lifespan of the motor car
as we know it today, and there can be very few family firms in the motor trade who can say
that in just two generations of adult motoring, and with the second generation
still firmly in control of the business, they can span these eventful years.
Robbins of Putney, who now operate an agency handling almost exclusively Rolls-Royce
and Bentley cars, is such a company, and has occupied its present premises
in Upper Richmond Road continuously since 1921.**

STANLEY THOMAS ROBBINS was born in 1880 at *The Elephant*, was educated at St Olaf's, and in 1897, by which time he had developed an interest in electrical engineering and photography, he took lodgings in the

Sheffield home of steel magnate Joseph R Bramah. Bramahs specialised in the fabrication of sheet metal, petrol tanks, mudguards and other items for motor manufacturers in the then new-found industry, and, later,

during the 1914 War, they also made aircraft parts. Encouraged by Mr Bramah, and probably because of these close associations with motor

Stanley Robbins at the wheel of his first car, an 8hp Decauville, photographed in about 1903.

7

manufacture, Stanley built himself a motorcycle in Bramah's courtyard at their home in Taptonville Road, Sheffield, utilising a single cylinder De Dion Bouton engine. This machine first took to the road *circa* 1898, but despite this promising beginning, it was to be upon electrical engineering and contract work that Stanley concentrated, and in 1900 he moved to Evesham, although both he and Bramah maintained contact thereafter.

By 1908 he was conducting electrical and photographic experiments, was installing electric lighting in houses and had commenced working on motor cars, and in that year he married. In 1910, Norman Stanley was born, and in 1913 his second son, Sidney Thomas, followed, at Evesham. Very shortly afterwards, Mr and Mrs Bramah visited them in an under-floor engined James and Browne, which had been acquired in 1910.

1913 also signalled the removal of the family to Wimbledon, where Stanley became General Manager of the St George's Motor Co, Kensington, and in Merton Road, Wandsworth, under the direction of a Mr Good. This firm was later taken over by Stearns of Brompton Road, and the Merton Road premises were eventually taken over by Joseph Lucas.

The outbreak of war in 1914 as usual found the army unprepared, and the Government seconded Stanley to commandeer civilian vehicles for army use, and it was not until 1921 that he had the opportunity to commence his own business. The Westminster Bank at Wandsworth had foreclosed on the premises at 96-98 Upper Richmond Road following the bankruptcy of the previous occupants, and with the help of the bank manager, Mr Morrish, Stanley was able to purchase these premises from the bank. It was intended that the Robbins family should live above the business premises, and to this end the family house at Wimbledon was sold in 1921. Unfortunately, however, there was no suitable living accommodation available, and whilst the premises were being converted, it was necessary for Stanley's wife, Sidney and Norman to move with their grandmother to a rented house at Herne Bay for six months or so.

In his capacity as an electrical engineer specialising in car electrics Stanley Robbins drove a wide variety of vehicles. This is a *circa* 1905 Maudslay with an early partner, Percy Hunt, in the back.

A 1905 single cylinder 8hp Cadillac with Worcestershire registration dating from Stanley Robbins' days in Evesham.

The Bramahs came from Sheffield to visit the Robbins in 1910 in this James and Browne horizontal underfloor engined model shown near Broadway Tower.

This move was accomplished in a lorry which Stanley converted from a *circa* 1912 Daimler landaulette, the conversion being carried out in the company's own coachworks.

Even following the move to Putney, the family still maintained their ties with Evesham, and it is an indication of the state of the roads at this relatively late date that on one eventful journey between Putney and Evesham in 1923, the large Cadillac which Stanley was using punctured no less than thirty spare tubes, and finally completed the journey with the last remaining cover stuffed with grass gathered from the roadside by ten-year-old Sidney and his elder brother.

In 1929 Sidney was apprenticed to the Malden Garage Co at Thelk Garage, Malden, in Essex. In these days, garages undertook their own work on tyres, and this establishment boasted an enormous steam operated tyre press. Sidney stayed on with the company for two years, latterly as stock manager, before moving to Henly's, where he remained during 1931-32.

Robbins Senior was a man of diverse interests, and in addition to electrical engineering and very early on during the Evesham days, as an adjunct to his experiments with photography, he began a series of tests with X-rays. Very little was known at that time other than the pioneer work carried out by Rontgen, and the result of these experiments was a very bad dose of radiation sickness! Stanley was forced to sit with his arms immersed in bowls of saline solution, kept at the correct temperature, but the treatment was successful and he recovered.

From the commencement of operations at Putney and until 1926, the company operated a coachbuilding workshop concerned mainly with commercial bodybuilding for vans, trucks and charabancs. This activity was under the direction of coach-builder Sid Hickman, who had previously been with Maudslay, whilst coachpainting was the province of a Mr Booth and Bert Matthews. The general adoption of cellulose sounded the deathknell of traditional coach-painting, but up until its introduction it was quite normal for Mr Booth to apply 22 coats (including two coats of varnish) to every finished job.

The staff were instructed to save,

religiously, all tea leaves, these being sprinkled by the bucketful on the floor of the coachbuilding shop to keep down the dust. Varnishing was invariably carried out at night, when there was little or no traffic in the street outside and less dust in the air.

The technique of coachpainting was an art practised with consummate skill by Mr Booth, and with his brush in his right hand, his small varnish pot between the forefinger and thumb of his left, he also carried a small, empty enamel mug on his little finger, in which to express all the air from the brush before the final 'laying off'. Cuttle-fish, as found on any English seaside beach, were also used. With the hard skin shredded off, and cut in half, they were used for the final rubbing down.

With everyone taking their job so seriously, it might be thought that the works were lacking in humour. High jinks were not unknown, however, and a favourite trick was to nail machinist Bill Davies' lunchtime apple to the work bench!

Hickman left the company in 1926, and at that stage coachbuilding was phased out. In the same year, labour unrest resulted in the General Strike, and with all public transport out of action, Stanley fitted bench seats in the back of the works' Talbot lorry, and used this to pick up his staff and bring them to work. His secretary, Miss Robinson (from the Pitman school), came from Battersea, and the Talbot ran the gauntlet of stones thrown by striking workers when collecting her from that area.

Like most small firms during that period, Robbins were practically self-sufficient, and their small workshops in the old stables at the rear of 96-98 Upper Richmond Road were able to cope with a variety of processes. All bearings were re-metalled and gear cutting was undertaken in the works which boasted a milling machine, lathe and forge with a compressor and large capacity gas pipe running on town gas. This formidable combination was capable of producing a tongue of flame four feet long! Putting his experience of house lighting to good effect (and having already electrified Bretforton Manor at Evesham for Squire Bretforton, using a Petter generator - he also supplied the Squire with a 1912 Cadillac

A 1913 Delage double landaulette with the unusual feature of a step to help in placing luggage on the roof.

15/18hp Swift of c1912 delivered to clothier Eric Abernathie of Ealing and photographed here at Studland Bay near Swanage.

This uncommon 1913 Napier is probably the four cylinder 16/22hp model. Its height is emphasised by the erected Auster screen.

limousine) he installed his own lighting plant at Putney in 1921, utilising a Delco system running on paraffin, and from that time onwards until mains electricity was installed, the company generated its own power.

During the twenties, agencies were secured for Austin, Humber, Triumph, Standard, Wolseley and Rover, and during these early days Stanley was very friendly with oil man Alexander Duckham, becoming one of the first retailers of Duckham's oils. At this time it was not unusual for motor manufacturers to have their own branded oil (usually produced for them by one of the major oil companies) and Duckhams produced one for William Morris, called Morrisol. It was also the period for gimmicks, and one of Duckham's less successful products were Adcoids. These were intended to act as an upper cylinder

lubricant, were waxy and about the size of a sugar lump, and were dropped into the petrol tank at the rate of one for every two gallons. Unfortunately, they tended to sink to the bottom of the tank, blocking the outlet pipe before dissolving, and in Mark II form were aerated so that they would float.

Brilliant engineer and mechanic though he was, Stanley was no businessman, and in the early days profits ran at little more than £200 p.a. His favourite saying was 'the word "can't" died in this family years ago!' and he was loathe ever to turn a job down, even when it was evident that

Converted from a Talbot 12/30 landaulette, this truck had an economy device in the shape of an air bleed on the manifold which could be opened from the dashboard when the engine was warm. Ex-despatch rider Ted Day used the Talbot for picking up staff during the General Strike, and had his windscreen broken by a mob for his trouble.

From their establishment at Putney in 1921 until 1926, Robbins had a coachbuilding department under the supervision of Sid Hickman. This is their work on a Model T.

A 1914 Arrol-Johnston 15.9hp tourer sold when secondhand from Robbins' Upper Richmond Road garage.

the work was totally unprofitable. In two notable cases involving a Straker-Squire and a Sheffield-Simplex, this enthusiasm ended in legal battles with difficult owners! Nevertheless, the business expanded steadily, and in 1929 a new showroom was purpose-built in Woodlands Way, just around the corner.

Although Sidney had helped his father from time to time in the business, and at an early age became used to holding the lead light whilst Robbins Senior worked late into the night beneath his Theophile Schneider, he did not join the family firm upon leaving Henly's at the end

of 1932. Instead, in 1933, both he and Norman joined a shoestring enterprise with more enthusiasm than prudence called RAG Carburettors, the name being derived from that of the redoubtable proprietress, Miss R A Garstin. Such business as the company was able to attract was conducted from premises in Tooting, and was managed by an irascible Irishman named Morris.

Norman and Sidney were taken on as testers, and one of the first large contracts which the company obtained was for the supply of carburettors to SS cars. RAGs were also used on Maseratis and OMs, and Dick Oates

In marked contrast to the coal scuttle bonneted Arrol-Johnston shown earlier is this 1924 15.9hp taxi landaulette supplied by Robbins.

One of the cars brought in for mechanical attention was this c1914 Sheffield-Simplex, which caused the firm endless aggravation and no profit.

of Rawlences, the OM concessionaires, was technical adviser to RAG.

Morris brought three Maseratis over from Italy to publicise the company's products, and a gentleman named Boyce from Hove also put a good deal of money into the business. When contracts came in - which wasn't often - and in those fine days before lines of demarcation were rigidly enforced by trade unions, everyone (including office girls) was transferred to the assembly lines and would work during the night, sometimes from 1am to 7.30 in the morning in order to meet delivery dates. The company's reserves were, at all times, slender, and that they managed to fulfil their obligations at all now seems a miracle. As no delivery van was owned by the company, Sidney was despatched in a decrepit two seater Clyno with 500 carburettors in the dickey seat in a mad overnight dash to Standard at Canley!

Charles Follett's Alvis 12/50 was also used to test the RAG, but attempts to achieve 100 mph consistently failed. Alterations increasing the choke size from 26mm to 28mm, and enlarging the main jets and power jets by 20cc had no effect, and Oates then suggested using BP No 4 Dope fuel. The attempt ended in disaster, since the car caught fire, as the carburettor float chamber had not been secured down properly. All good things come to an end, and by 1936 the luckless Morris had run Miss Garstin and RAG deeply into the red, and unable to see his way out of this morass, the poor fellow shot himself in a taxi at Vauxhall.

Sidney then joined his father at

Bought and sold by Stanley Robbins was this bizarre Szawe made by Szabo and Wechselmann of Berlin - coachbuilders who had turned motor makers in 1920. The radiator surround was hammered German silver and the body was wood and copper. Its 2.5 litre engine was apparently totally gutless.

1924 sleeve valve Minerva 15 doctor's coupé supplied by Robbins about 1924 and shown here in Carlton Drive, Putney.

New premises were opened at Woodlands Way in 1929 and this unusual sportsman's coupé bodied Morris was photographed outside its Buick and Clyno showroom windows.

Putney, and Norman joined Robin Jackson at Brooklands, but later, having had enough of the motor trade, joined the Stone Platt Group, with whom he stayed until he retired.

Stanley was very friendly with Mr F Batten, a cycle maker in Cullompton in Devon reputed to be the owner of the first motor car in Devon (and later area distributor for Austin), and during various visits to the Batten premises, young Sidney met the daughter of the house, who was in charge of her father's office, and in August 1936 he married her.

The Vauxhall concession was taken

One of their most successful agencies was for Humber and here we see a 1928 14/40 tourer supplied to a Mr H Morrison with his chauffeur Ernest Wood at the wheel.

A view of the Woodlands Way showrooms in the early thirties with Citroën, Swift 10 and Napier breakdown truck in the foreground and Hillman, Humber and many more behind.

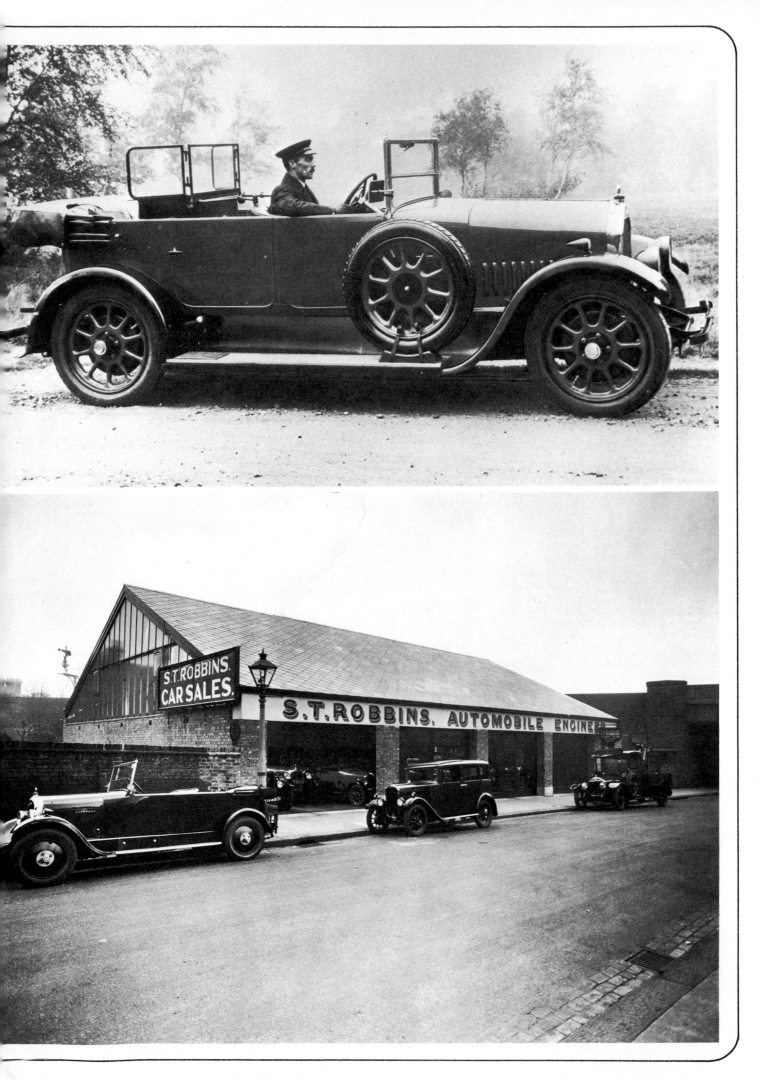

on in 1934 and not relinquished until 1968, and the company also handled Studebakers from 1936 to 1938. With the outbreak of war in 1939, Robbins of Putney Ltd were entrusted under the Essential Works Order of 1939 with the maintenance of essential transport, and until 1946 were busily engaged in ambulance conversion, the building of mobile canteens and the maintenance of ambulances and doctors' cars. An interesting job undertaken at this time was to rebuild the Czechoslovakian Aero drophead coupé owned by Doctor Benesch, the Czech Ambassador, who was based at Putney. Collected in several tea chests, it was successfully re-assembled and the car was the subject of an article by D B 'Bunny' Tubbs in *The Motor*.

Stanley retired in 1944 and Sidney became Managing Director, but with the return to normality in 1946, times were difficult, and with most new cars going for export, customers awaiting new vehicles had to be prepared for a three year wait. To prevent profiteering on new cars, the Motor Agents Association introduced their Covenant Scheme, under the terms of which customers agreed that, having received delivery of their new car, they would not sell it until a given period had expired.

As conditions improved, further expansion took place, and in 1948 the company acquired 84 Upper Richmond Road with a 3000 square foot building for housing new cars and a car park area surrounding it, and in 1956 extensive alterations were carried out to the showroom at the main premises. During the course of rebuilding, it was found that the beams supporting the previous showroom floor were resting on a ledge only ½ins wide, and it was a wonder that the entire contents had not previously collapsed into the basement!

Following the takeover of Rootes Group by Chrysler, the company relinquished the Humber concession which it had held since the 1920s, and latterly began to concentrate more and more upon Rolls-Royce and Bentley cars. Stanley died in 1968, by which time difficulties in obtaining sufficient deliveries of Rovers, and increasing warranty claims on the several BMC

Two years later in 1950 this is what some of their most popular lines consisted of - Standard Vanguard, Rover 75, Wolseley 4/50, Vauxhall Velox, Austin Devon and Morris Oxford.

Some 1956 bargains in Robbins' recently modernised Putney premises, including Jaguar, Rover, Ford and Mercedes.

Robbins sold Vauxhalls from 1934 to 1968 and this is their showroom, suitably decorated, in 1957 for that panel beater's nightmare, the Victor.

(later British Leyland) products which the company handled, eventually brought about the decision in 1976 to concentrate solely upon Rolls-Royce and Bentley, and to drop all other agencies.

The premises at 84 Upper Richmond Road were sold in 1972, and those in Woodlands Way more recently, leaving a more compact and streamlined business specialising in Rolls-Royce and Bentley to be carried on at the original premises, with workshops at the rear. After 60 years, the company has earned itself an enviable reputation, and conducts its business on an international level, the Rolls and Bentley connections having been recently strengthened by the arrival of Brian Blowers as Managing Director; previously Managing Director of Lex Mead, Weybridge, and Director of Mann Egerton, Rolls-Royce and Bentley specialists.

For those with a sense of history, and remembering how Henry Royce first became involved in the building of motor cars, it is interesting to contemplate that one of Stanley Robbins' earliest cars was a Decauville very similar to that which Henry Royce owned and set out to improve in 1903.

THE CURRENT SCENE

Star in the East. This is the actual No 2 car entered by Star of Wolverhampton in the 1905 Gordon Bennett Eliminating Trials. It later went to India and all trace of it was lost for over seventy years. 1978/9 saw its rediscovery - in derelict but virtually complete condition - and re-importation into Britain. Fully restored, it has had a full rally season in the hands of new owner Nick Ridley of the Veteran Car Club.

DESPITE all the rumblings about impending fuel shortages and the energy crisis, enthusiasm for early vehicles has continued on a rising tide during the year with rallies plentiful and well attended and the London-Brighton (as always) over-subscribed.

Rising prices were highlighted (but not typified) by the US $440,000 paid for a 500K Mercedes Benz at Christie's Los Angeles Auction in February and in the world record £4600 achieved by a 1927 Austin Seven Chummy (admittedly a Beau-

Fifty years ago. This 1924 Bullnosed Cowley, seen here photographed in 1928, was not destined for a thirties scrapyard like so many of its contemporaries. Laid up in an old fish curing shed in Sheringham, Norfolk, with an almost identical second car in 1929, it was rediscovered [with its twin] absolutely intact and original [even down to 1929 tax disc] by the Editor this year.

lieu concours winner) at Sotheby's in April, but prophets of doom who warn us that the supply of old cars will soon 'dry up', however, continue to be confounded, and a healthy crop of original and unrestored cars continues to surface.

Latest discoveries of importance falling into this category include Nick Ridley's 1905 Gordon Bennett 70hp Star racer (the No 2 team car), found derelict, but virtually complete and hardly used, in India, and since fully restored in Great Britain; two entirely original and very complete Morris Cowley 'bullnosed' tourers of 1924 vintage, found by your editor in a fish curing warehouse in Sheringham, Norfolk, where they had lain since 1929/30, and a 1909 Type LA 2 45hp Sheffield-Simplex, found minus back axle (which incorporated the gearbox) and in chassis form only, in Australia, but which has now been re-imported into Britain and is being rebuilt in its native Sheffield. A host of lesser discoveries would seem to indicate that there is still plenty left to find if you dig deep enough.

Worldwide, the economic climate has had its effect on the movement as a whole, and America, particularly, has suffered. This has resulted in an encouraging influx of vehicles back into Britain - a reversal of the trend in

years past - but leaves the American enthusiasts the poorer. Auction houses Stateside have also suffered - Kruse, the largest, reporting heavy losses and apparently experiencing difficulty in making payment to vendors. If money is short, however, enthusiasm is not lacking and one old car newspaper reports 100,000 readers weekly. Britain seems over the worst of her trade recession problems and the future augurs well for 1980 which will be another milestone - the fiftieth anniversary of the founding of The Veteran Car Club of Great Britain - which will be suitably celebrated with a mammoth jubilee rally.

All in all, it's been a good year, and if by the time you read this the much talked-about scrapping of the Road Fund Licence has become a reality, then 1980 could be even better. With Swansea relieved of most of the duties which they were expensively set up to provide, perhaps they could devote some time to sorting out the mountains of early registration documentation which, we are told, is piled in aircraft hangars around the country, and have it re-distributed to sympathetic county archivists or the Public Record Office. Certainly it would be a tragedy if these early records were to be lost, particularly as some enlightened local authorities took the trouble to preserve the remainder rather than send them to Swansea in the first place.

AT THE KERBSIDE

It seems that, even in Spain and parts of South America which were previously rich hunting grounds, most of the early vehicles have disappeared. Just to prove that there are some oases left, however, GEORGE AVRAMIDIS and MR AND MRS BART VANDERVEEN have been kerbside car gazing in Athens, Spain, France and Colombia, and the following photographs illustrate some of their discoveries.

IT doesn't seem so long ago that a half hour spent wandering round the more run-down bed-sit areas of Kensington, Earls Court and Belgravia would produce a handsome crop of vintage cars of all types standing at the kerb. Many of them were semi-abandoned, others in daily use, whilst the rest were patiently awaiting the day when their impecunious owners could scrape up the cash for another three months road tax or a third party insurance at £6.5.3d. Almost without exception,

they were scruffy, and run by penniless enthusiasts and students who liked them, or simply by those who could not afford anything newer.

In Spain and Provincial France it was much the same story except that the traditional frugality of these agricultural areas seemed to have evolved a foolproof method of keeping vehicles running in a state of utter neglect and near disintegration. Market day in any French country district would inevitably produce its

crop of down-at-heel Citroëns, a Brasier camionette, perhaps, or a Rochet-Schneider cut down into a truck, and all heavily overloaded with pigs, goats and chickens.

Perhaps the oldest style vehicle still in regular production in Spain is the 80 ins wheelbase Universal Jeep. Nowadays known as the Jeep Bravo, this is, in fact, the 1952 pattern Willys CJ3B. Until a few years ago it was a product of the VIASA division of CAF and known as the CJ3, but it is now one of the many vehicle types sold by the rapidly expanding Motor Iberica concern, and is only available with the Spanish made Perkins 4.108 diesel engine. In addition to the Bravo, there are the long wheelbase Bravo L (previously the CJ6) with the same front end styling, the Commando (originally the American Jeepster of 1967) and the SV range (Spanish forward control truck, van, bus, etc) on 2.56 metre wheelbase with Perkins 4.203 engine.

Doctors seem to favour pre-war vehicles in Athens. This *circa* 1934/35 Morris Eight tourer is in everyday use.

Apart from a rather soft rear tyre, this 1925 Fiat 509F appears eminently restorable and complete, even down to hood and sidescreens. It appears to be currently in use in Athens.

This *circa* 1935 Studebaker Commander looks remarkably complete and sound despite the neglect and would appear to be still working for its living in Athens.

Greek pick-a-back: this 1938 Vauxhall 14hp saloon is obviously 'going the journey'. A pity, since it seems bodily quite sound and complete.

Rara Avis. The home-made Greek grille doesn't disguise the fact that this is the German version of the Ford 10 - the Eiffel, with 1157cc sv engine which preceded the Taunus. Dating from *circa* 1938, this one has non-original wheels.

The bodywork is 1940 De Soto SP9 sedan but the cart-sprung beam type front axle could mean either light truck chassis or re-axled [not unusual]. Note the missing rear wing and the substitute radiator grille. By the wayside is a late 1960s Kaiser Jeep Jeepster station wagon. Light 4x4 vehicles are very common in Colombia with many makes and models represented.

Axis survivor: not only British WWII vehicles survive in Greece. This is a much modified VW Kubelwagen still giving good service.

Offered only in 'six light' saloon form, this postwar [*circa* 1946] Series M Morris Ten was well known for its unburstable engine, lively handling and well chosen gear ratios. This one, in Athens, with non-original winkers and sidelights is looking a little the worse for wear.

This 1938 Hudson 112 evokes fond memories for the Editor. He bought one for £3.10.0d. and ran it for a week minus sump! This quite respectable example was photographed in Athens.

Not all Athenian survivors are in poor condition. This trim and original 1946 Plymouth De Luxe two door coupé is kept in excellent condition by its doctor owner.

This *circa* 1945 little Sunbeam Talbot 10 is characterised by 'four light' appearance in a 'six light' car, there being no pillar to the rear of the rear door mountings. This one seems to have been giving its Greek owner some trouble, but at least boasts a starting handle.

Another Athenian survivor from WWII? This apparently ex-military AP Austin 8hp is in remarkably complete and original condition - a pity about the front hub cap.

'It only hurts when I smile.' The 'Blind Pew' effect of this 1946 De Soto De Luxe sorts ill with the brave mouth organ grin so typical of the period. Obviously, someone in Athens still cares, however, if the chains on the door handles are any indication.

It is difficult to say whether this is a *circa* 1946 Triumph 1800 or the later 2000 with Standard Vanguard engine. The original semaphore signals seem to have been blocked in [just aft of the doors] and the rear light cluster is non-original, but otherwise it appears to have weathered well in the Greek climate.

This 1948 Vauxhall Wyvern, reflecting its pre-war ancestry, is obviously still in use in Athens and looks quite clean.

Chevrolet Fleetmaster DK2103 sedan of 1946 vintage, sporting a modified ex-Dodge truck radiator grille of the early seventies. Note ill-fitting bonnet and wings as a result of crude accident repairs. Bumper is not original but cars are kept running regardless in Colombia.

What appears to be another abandoned car in the Athens area. It wasn't so long ago that these 'traction avant Citroën 11CVs' abounded in France. Immortalised by Maigret, they were extensively used by the French police. This one ekes out its last days somewhere near Athens.

Battered 1947 Ford Fordor sedan, still going strong. Noteworthy are the cross-country tyres with stick-on white sidewalls. Most vehicles have only one windscreen wiper and even that is likely to be 'lifted' when car is left unattended in Colombia.

Obviously abandoned and only one step from the Greek breaker's torch, this 1949 Nash Custom is a rare bird outside its native America.

LIFE & DEATH ON THE BOARDS

51-20

There was a period, twenty years at the outset, but mostly crammed into a single decade, when America's most spectacular auto racing took place on huge wooden oval tracks, with curves so steeply banked that the Board Speedways became known as 'saucers'. Perhaps a quarter of a billion board feet of edge-on 2 x 4s went into the construction of the roughly two dozen tracks that sprung up across the country following World War I. Compared to the road racing popular in Europe, these giant arenas provided totally artificial conditions, but also the impetus for the development of supercharging, streamlining, front wheel drive and long-lived engine stamina - all part of the specification of many of today's most advanced automobiles. FREDERICK A USHER takes a backward look at America's board racing era.

And they're off. The pace car [a Mercer?] has pulled over and car no 12, Jimmy Murphy's Duesenberg has edged in front of Thomas' Frontenac.

JUST a few miles from the site where America's first Board Track had been built ten years earlier, the new Los Angeles Speedway, located on a vast plot of undeveloped land that would later become Beverly Hills, was the most 'posh' of the fabulous Speedway Era tracks. On Thanksgiving Day, 25th November 1920, an estimated 75,000 spectators - including California socialites and Hollywood celebrities, glittering with diamonds, according to contemporary accounts - mingled in the elegant covered grandstand and watched a pre-race spectacular put on by the 'air service' from March Field. The following day the newspaper said, 'We're never going to have another war, of course, but to see the pilots doing impossible stunts was something like being given a big insurance policy'. (One senses a whiff of intended irony, as though the commentator wasn't quite buying the popular post-war cliché.)

Leaning nonchalantly against their Duesenberg are the ill-fated driver and mechanic, O'Donnell and Jolls [reports of the race give differing spellings of their names].

Also in the Duesenberg team that day were Eddie Miller and Stu Wilkinson [standing] who were to finish second at an average speed of 102 mph.

A spectator's eye view of the great wooden saucer showing the steep banking and some of the competitors, as well as Barney Oldfield's pace car.

As the spectators craned their heads skyward, noted race photographer Hughes tripped the shutter of his panorama camera for a broad picture of the entire line-up of drivers, mechanics, pit men and race officials. The resulting image of divided attention has a strange, vacant quality (and cannot be reproduced) - even further, weird though it may have seemed later - by some ominous quirk of fate, ace driver Eddie O'Donnell's image was blotted out by an adjacent photographer's tripod leg!

Then, while some of the more elite race fans indulged themselves with gourmet box lunches of turkey with cranberry sauce and mince pie, Hughes lugged his heavy camera down the line-up for individual pictures of racecars and crews - catching O'Donnell grinning through a sandwich, and his 'mechanician' Jolls jauntily dangling a cigarette. Their casual confidence may have hidden deeper moods, as suggested by a reminiscence of spectator Lawrence H Nelson:

'The day before the race I was in the pits, and Chevrolet and O'Donnell seemed not too friendly. It seemed O'Donnell was not too happy with the way his car was running. Gaston said, "We will run the Duesenbergs off the track". O'Donnell said, "That we will have to see". O'Donnell was very peeved. I know, because I tried on his leather helmet, and he blew his stack, and told me it was a bad omen.'

'Racing obviously is madness. For one thing it is quite lethally dangerous.' So begins the first chapter of the Old Testament of American auto racing - Griff Borgeson's *Golden Age of the American Racing Car*. Before launching into his history, Borgeson gives us two concise pages of pungent words on the individual psychological motivations for racing, the social symbolism of the activity, and its final material manifestation in the pure bred machine. Briefly brushed is the 'gamble with death', for - just as the *aficionado* of the bullring is bored with elaborate explanations of the ceremony - the racing enthusiast is uncomfortable with a discussion of the 'final and inevitable'. When it strikes there is disbelief and trauma. Such was the overpowering mood following the Thanksgiving Day race at the Los Angeles Speedway. Earlier races of

that 1920 season had developed the competitive context that culminated in the tragic accident which claimed the lives of Gaston Chevrolet and Eddie O'Donnell that November afternoon over a half-century ago. For a proper perspective on the 1920 season it is necessary to look at the few previous years.

Pre-WWI racing activities in Europe ended with the famous 1914 Grand Prix at Lyon, which took place only a few weeks before the outbreak of hostilities, but the only immediate effect of the war on the American scene was the drying up of competition from Europe. This potential loss of interest worried the Indianapolis Speedway management and caused them to take a bold step - one that was almost unprecedented in the history of auto racing. Unable to obtain new cars from Europe, the Speedway simply commissioned the construction, by an American firm, of three brand new copies of the highly successful French Peugeot. Peugeot had produced the first 'modern' high performance engine, one incorporating the basic features of today's racing engines.

Racing continued through the 1916 season, and resumed again in 1919.

The eventual winner, Roscoe Sarles, in Duesenberg 10 overtakes Eddie Miller's Duesie on the straight in front of the stands.

For 1920, regulations reduced engine size to a maximum of 183 cu in to bring them into line with the European limit of 3 litres. It was expected that performance would suffer, compared with the previous 300 cu in cars and, worse, there were fears about the reliability of new, untried designs.

As the time approached for the Memorial Day race at Indianapolis, the Duesenberg brothers were desperately trying to complete their 183 cu in straight eights, basically scaled down versions of their 1919 cars. In France, Ballot had taken the same route, producing smaller capacity versions of his 1919 machines, essentially eight cylinder Peugeots, one of which had been campaigned in the US by Ralph DePalma. The Chevrolet brothers with Cornelius van Ranst had produced an all new design, but even these cars, running as *Frontenac* and *Monroe* - with the only difference being paint colour - derived a great deal from the classic pre-war Peugeot. The Chevrolet cars were put together like jewellery and, through the liberal use of aluminium and new steel alloys, were very light. Peugeot fielded three cars of completely new design - notable only for the inexplicable use of three camshafts operating no less than 5 valves per cylinder. Predictably, all retired from the race with 'engine trouble', and seem never to have been heard from again.

De Palma's Ballot was quite the fastest machine present, leading the qualifiers at 99.15 mph, and except for his proverbial bad luck, De Palma should have won easily. In spite of a bad start after visiting his pit on the first lap because of tyre trouble, by 150 miles De Palma had the Ballot in second place behind Boyer, whose *Frontenac* had been the fastest of the seven Chevrolet cars. At the 300 mile mark, the Ballot was in front and piling up a healthy lead, but with only 14 laps to go, one of the two magnetos cut out and De Palma limped home on four cylinders, thankful for fifth place.

If bad luck spoiled De Palma's race, miraculous good luck gave victory to Gaston Chevrolet, whose *Frontenac* crossed the line first, four minutes ahead of Thomas' Ballot. One by one, each after approximately 550 miles of use, the steering arms on Louis Chevrolet's Monroe/Frontenac cars snapped, and the little cars crashed out of control - twice with courageous Roscoe Sarles at the wheel, once in his Monroe, and a second time while driving relief in Bennett Hill's Frontenac. The steering arm on Gaston's car, the last to be assembled and with no time for practice, survived the race only to fall apart in the garage when Louis angrily kicked a front wheel!

Later in the season De Palma finally drove his Ballot to victory in the Elgin Road Race but as the time approached for the big Thanksgiving Day race at the 'Beverly Hills Board Track', on points, Gaston Chevrolet was still the man to beat. In spite of their notoriously casual machining standards, which usually resulted in damaged valve gear, the Duesenbergs had accumulated an impressive record on the board tracks: winning the inaugural at Beverly Hills in February, Uniontown in June and September, Tacoma in July and Fresno in October. Tommy Milton was runner-up in AAA points, with 930 to Gaston's 1030 (later, given contested points for win(s) at Uniontown, Milton became AAA champion for 1920) but, because of the 'Daytona incident', Milton, who was the best of the Duesenberg drivers, left the team late in the season to campaign Durant's Miller-built 'Chevrolet Special' which had been re-engined

with a Duesenberg straight eight.

So - for this final event of the 1920 season at the Los Angles Speedway, competition was strong among the Duesenberg drivers, and Eddie O'Donnell, who had been running behind Milton and Murphy most of the season, must have been especially eager. Newspaper reports stated, 'Eddie probably worked harder in an effort to get his Duesenberg in shape than any other driver in the field. He was up early and late tinkering in the shop to get his mount tuned perfectly ...', but with hindsight, added ' ... misfortune has followed him and he has suffered many mishaps, some only affecting the mechanical operation of his car, it is true, but nearly always just when victory seemed almost within his grasp'.

The Race - edited from a contemporary report:
'It was exactly 1.30 when Starter Frederick Wagner and Referee Eddie Rickenbacker called the drivers to the

Part of the fashionable Beverly Hills crowd with their autos having a clear view of fourth man Eddie Hearne in the Revere Special.

Close-up of Eddie Hearne with mechanic Hartz before the race. Revere [or Re-Vere] speedsters were built at Logansport for a short time at the end of the Great War with Rochester-Duesenberg engines].

line, with Barney Oldfield in the lead as pacemaker for the preliminary lap. There was a word from the starter and they were away, rolling around the big oval at a seventy mile clip.

'Coming into the straight, approaching the starting line, they were lined up almost perfectly and Wagner gave them the chequered flag. Away they went!

'As the cars flashed by the numbers were checked off - but where was O'Donnell? There was a roar and Eddie came by with a rush. With his heart in the race and out to win, he took advantage of his supposedly poor position last in line to hang back, and

Furious at being outdriven by team mate Sarles, O'Donnell presses on recklessly on the heels of Gaston Chevrolet in his Frontenac.

Furious at being outdriven by team mate Sarles, O'Donnell presses on recklessly on the heels of Gaston Chevrolet in his Frontenac.

O'Donnell hurtles past the pits ahead of Hearne on the 45th lap.

then sped up with a clear field while the others were packing up in the short stretch to the first turn.

'Eddie's scheme gave him a tremendous start into the curve and by the seventeenth lap he had climbed from last into second position, only a short distance behind the leading Duesie with Sarles at the wheel. From then on, O'Donnell was in the running and near the top until he went to the pits in his fifty-sixth lap with a broken rocker arm, practically eliminated. The repair cost him 15 minutes, 42 seconds. It was his only stop until his accident in the 138th lap, but it put him back in sixth or seventh place despite his desperate efforts to pick up.

'Murphy, driving Duesenberg No 12, drew the pole and led the field at the end of the first and third laps, see-sawing with Sarles for the honour, but the latter let his car out a notch and from the fourth on was never in serious danger, and declared after it was all over that had it been necessary his car would have turned up an average two or three miles an hour better.

'Tommy Milton, who was second only to Chevrolet at the start of the event in championship points, had the hard luck to break a valve stem in his 22nd lap and was out of the race for good.

'Brushes that thrilled the stands time and again occurred all through from early in the race. Milton, Thomas, Thiele and Miller were bunched for lap after lap and fought it out for position at one or another extremity of the course, while Sarles, O'Donnell and Murphy, laps in the lead, staged their own individual battles at the opposite end. At no time were there more than four cars in a bunch and it was largely due to this fact that the tragic accident involved only the two cars.

'Murphy suffered hard luck early in the race and only desperate work on his part brought him up to the finish in fourth place. In the thirty-first lap he was out for three minutes for a right rear tyre and dirty spark plugs. In the very next lap he was in again, this time for ignition trouble, losing a minute and a half.

'With the race three-fourths gone, he was compelled to stop again, this time for a right front tyre. This was but a brief stop, however, for the change was made in the fast time of fifteen seconds flat. The real record for tyre change came to Eddie Hearne, who switched a wrecked right front for a new one in fourteen seconds flat, just after completing his ninety-first lap.

'The lap time perhaps was one of the most remarkable features of the event. With mile and a quarter circuits time after time turned in 42-3/5 and 42-4/5 seconds, between 105 and 106 miles an hour, it seemed early in the game as if the pilots were out to chop off a big hunk from the mark set by the 300 cubic inch cars back in February.'

From the fourth lap, Roscoe Sarles in Duesenberg No 10 had led all the way. As the three-quarter mark passed, *Los Angeles Examiner* staff photographer Billy Stapp was standing on the hood of an automobile parked at the east turn of the Speedway. 'Several laps before the fatal one, I noticed that the cars battling for the lead (Miller and Hearne) skidded badly when rounding the turn. I felt there was to be an accident and on the lap before it occurred I picked Chevrolet and watched him speed around the track. As Chevrolet and O'Donnell passed the grandstand I saw they were fighting hard for position. I focused my camera on them as they came to the turn. As soon as I saw Chevrolet swing up toward O'Donnell, I snapped my camera.'

Billy Stapp's photo appeared on the front page of next day's *Los Angeles Examiner*, along with an account of the accident, somewhat less sober than the race account quoted above:

'The Goddess of Speed took her toll yesterday from those who follow in her train. While 75,000 persons came to their feet in a shuddering gasp, two racing automobiles collided at blinding speed and rolled from the top of the Los Angeles Speedway to the field below. Death was with them as they rolled.

'Gaston Chevrolet was killed instantly. Life was extinct when he was lifted from the wreck of his Frontenac. Lyall Jolles, mechanician in the Duesenberg No 9, was sent hurling over the fence at the top of the track and fell thirty feet to the ground outside the Speedway. He lived but a few minutes.

'Eddie O'Donnell, driver of the Duesenberg, late last night was in critical condition at the California hospital, with a compound fracture of the skull, a broken arm and possible internal injuries.

'Of the four men who rode the ill fated cars, but one escaped. On Johnnie Bresnahan, mechanician for Chevrolet, perverse Fate chose to smile. Though knocked unconscious, he came through the appalling crash marked only by two small scratches.'

Details of the action leading to the accident were reported by the newspaper as follows:

'Chevrolet was on his 147th lap. He was attempting to pass Joe Thomas, who was slightly ahead in his Frontenac. At the same time, O'Donnell was pursuing Chevrolet. The three

cars thundered past the pits, with Chevrolet and O'Donnell gaining. The spectators cheered the spirited brush.

'As they climbed the last bank, Chevrolet picked up speed and made the effort to pass Thomas, below him. Simultaneously, O'Donnell began to pass the Duesenberg. The cars were inches apart.

'Bresnahan, mechanician for Chevrolet, was looking back and, seeing that O'Donnell was trying to pass, beckoned him to come on.

'But just as the Duesenberg swept past, Chevrolet's wheel was seen to twist, ever so little, to the right. The Frontenac swerved an inch or two, perhaps, but enough to cause its right front wheel to touch O'Donnell's car near the driver's seat.

'Chaos followed. Thomas flew by on the left, untouched. But O'Donnell's car was catapulted in a semi-circle

ahead of Chevrolet. It might, perhaps, have righted itself but its swerve placed it directly in the path of the Frontenac and this time Chevrolet's car hit it, head on and directly in the middle.

'The Duesenberg was hurled up the track until it struck the fence, smashing about thirty feet of the stout timbers to matchwood. So strong was the obstacle, however, that the car bounded back and started its roll, over and over down that terrible incline - with but one occupant. Jolles, the mechanician, was thrown forward by the crash and, rising in a horrible arc, he completely cleared the fence and dived thirty feet to his death, outside the Speedway.

'Meanwhile, Chevrolet's car, recoiling from the second collision, turned turtle and was rolling, ahead of the Duesenberg, down the boards to the dirt at the border of the track. With a smash that was plainly audible above the roar of thunderous exhausts, the cars brought up against the bottom fence.'

Shocked by the appalling accident, Peter De Paolo later commented on the incident in his autobiography *Wall Smacker*:

'The track officials agreed that it was Eddie's terrible temper that caused the wreck. Eddie was supposed to be the star of the Duesenberg team. Sarles had just recently joined Duesenberg, after driving a Chevrolet-built Monroe in the Indianapolis race the previous May. O'Donnell was peeved because his car was not right that day and when Sarles, a new member of the team, stepped out and trimmed him, it hurt his pride. Late in the race, after many stops, O'Donnell pulled out from his pit hopelessly beaten, and so mad that he became reckless. His car locked hubs with Gaston Chevrolet's car. Slam! With their wheels entangled they both hit the upper rail, ricocheted off, sliding down the steep embankment to the apron below.'

Photographer Hughes had covered the race action adequately, but when

the accident occurred was not in the advantageous position that intuition had given Billy Stapp. Hughes shot the mangled cars of O'Donnell and Chevrolet, and with these and other negatives of the race, he created his own wreck photo back in his studio.

The spectacular picture he produced, which shows winner Sarles flashing past the crumpled remains of the two ill fated cars, has been sometimes uncharitably denounced as a 'fake'. Actually, Hughes produced a montage, combining three separate negatives - very effective, say, in the small reproduction facing the passage quoted above from De Paolo's book - but a good print shows Hughes to have been more adept with a camera than with a brush.

Understandably, the terrible accident cast a pall over what might have been a classic race in the Golden Age. As expressed by the *Examiner* writers:

'It shocked to the depths one of the greatest throngs ever gathered in the West to view a sporting event .... and seriously marred what promised to be an ideal race, on an ideal day ... While the winner was given a hearty cheer when he flashed over the line, it was perhaps less hearty than had been given to him and others of the drivers earlier in the race for the mere passing of a rival.'

There were other races at the Los Angeles Speedway, and others died in perhaps even more appalling incidents. As the twenties roared on, one by one the Board Tracks were levelled by floods, fires and hurricanes, but mostly by the pressure of urban growth - itself an unforeseen effect of the automobile. Four years after the Chevrolet/O'Donnell crash, the finest of the Board Tracks, which had come to be known as the Beverly Hills Speedway, was gone. In its place there now stand row upon row of neatly manicured homes in the various eclectic pseudo styles preferred by the Southern Californian of the late nineteen twenties.

Of all the manifestations of the Roaring Twenties - Jazz, the Charleston, Bathtub Gin and Bootlegging, Hollywood movies - perhaps the Board Track 'speedfests' most perfectly symbolise the era. Mad as the phenomena may appear to some now, the great wooden saucers can also be seen as crucibles into which was poured the ingenuity and inventiveness which produced the durable tyres, hightest fuels and lubricants, and the mechanical perfection of the automobiles we drive today.

ARMSTRONG

**For some inexplicable reason Armstrong Siddeleys - and particularly those of the thirties -
have tended to be unloved by enthusiasts, and it is only relatively recently
that they have been 'brought in from the cold'. Quite why this should be so
is difficult to fathom, since the cars were well built although conservative, and
in sporting guise far from slow. MICHAEL SEDGWICK examines
the company's range during the decade leading up to the Second World War
and traces similarities with Packard - another proud independent
with strong aero engine background.**

'YOU Cannot Buy a Better Car,' proclaimed Armstrong Siddeley Motors in the 1930s.

It depended, of course, on what you wanted. It depended still more on whether your tastes coincided with John Davenport Siddeley's. It wasn't, perhaps, an accident that he chose the

inscrutable Sphinx as his emblem, but while he was loath to put a label on his cars he had strong ideas on how they should be driven. Preselector quadrants on four-speeders read 'Low-Medium-Normal-High', and he regarded bumpers (which he called 'buffers') as a sop to careless drivers,

hence they remained extras as late as 1933/34. He was totally uninterested in the mass market (his one sally into the bargain basement, the 1922 Stoneleigh, had been a monumental goof!). The inexpensive 12hp sports coupé was aimed at 'daughters of gentlemen' and at Parkside mass production

SIDDELEY

H.1103

This 1936 Siddeley Special Mark II boasts a Sports saloon body by Hooper and a non-original radiator mascot in place of the usual sphinx. This was the model driven to the South of France by Jack Barclay. Impressed, he indicated to Armstrong Siddeley that he would like the agency. Perhaps understandably, considering the similarity [outwardly at least] to their Phantom II Continental, Rolls-Royce threatened to cancel their agency if he went ahead, and that was that.

meant a commission (Siddeley, like Packard, never thought in model years) for a thousand identical chassis. Styling was almost as conservative as Packard's, though Siddeley progressed from vee to flat radiators before returning to vees for good. (The 'flats', in any case, were reserved for the under £400 class.) As for bodies, curves made their appearance in 1928,

and the inswept tail was first seen in 1932, but thereafter 'coach saloons' changed little right up to 1939.

There are other parallels. Both companies sold factory warranted used cars, and both were addicted to the disc wheel. Eight stud discs were standard on the first Siddeley of all, the 30hp of 1919; though latterly the studs were tucked away behind nave plates, such footwear was found on the vast majority of the company's products, even if bolt-on wires were an option throughout the 1930s. Armstrong Siddeley's one concession to aerodynamics was to lower the Sphinx onto his haunches, out of the draught. This modification was first seen on 1932 Twenties.

Engineering was likewise conservative. The Siddeley Special apart, there

were no dramatic breakthroughs in the decade, and changes spread so gradually down the range that they passed unnoticed. No pre-war Armstrong Siddeley had hydraulic brakes, and no cars with i.f.s. reached the public before 1945. On the credit side, of course, was the famous Wilson preselective gearbox, best of the semi-automatics, for all its muted banshee howls in neutral. It had been available on the biggest cars from late 1928, and would be standardised four years later. Since the quadrant merely selected the gears, its right-hand location never irritated as much as Standard's later column shifts, but the Wilson didn't like being hurried. On really big engines like the Siddeley Special's, the flywheel tended to become quarrelsome if an instant

September 1931, and the chauffeur demonstrates the new fold-away luggage grid fitted to the 20hp Sports saloon. Note the absence of reflectors and single rear lamp. The railway carriage type square-ended locking key would hardly meet the approval of today's crime prevention officer

downshift was essayed. Hence the short-lived fluid flywheel option of 1931-33; the fact that this didn't last long suggests either that Siddeley owners weren't in a hurry or that they trusted their Bendix brakes.

One shouldn't, of course, dismiss the whole tribe as ugly and gutless. The former charge could certainly be levelled at early 30s, with their aggressive vee shaped honeycombs and foursquare formal coachwork, unrelieved by any brightwork. But some of Cyril Siddeley's later creations possessed considerable charm - the much derided 12 coupé of 1934, for instance, or the four door Atalantas marketed between 1936 and 1938. Even the angular sports saloons of the early 1930s had a certain elegance, and were blessed with thin pillars in an era when driver vision was little considered. One is tempted to regard

this model as the true precursor of the razor-edge idiom; there are marked similarities with some of Freestone and Webb's prentice efforts on Derby Bentley chassis.

As for the stigma of refined gutlessness, this may be true of the 12/6. Certainly no Siddeley would stand a chance in the traffic-light Grand Prix. But the bigger ones possessed a performance entirely adequate for their class: a 3.2 litre Short 20 with maybe 70 bhp under its bonnet would top the 70 mark, cruise all day in the middle 60s, and reach 50 in 16.8 seconds, about the norm for a British car. Remember, too, that it turned the scales at 3864 pounds, as against 3450 for a contemporary Buick with 78 advertised brake horses. A similar performance could be extracted from the last pre-war 20/25 limousines, solid two tonners. Further, if Siddeley's quadrant labelling was a trifle dictatorial, it wasn't unjustified: the company offered a close ratio third in days when three bottoms and one top were only too common on British family saloons.

Sales remained healthy throughout

the decade: any fall-off after 1936 was the result of a growing demand for aero engines and not of any loss of owner confidence. Even in 1937, extensions were in hand at the Parkside factory to maintain deliveries in the face of rearmament. With the aid of the ASOC, I've been able to unearth some production figures: these show that 31,167 Armstrong Siddeleys were turned out between 1930 and 1939, an average of well over 3000 a year. Not bad, when one reflects that nothing ever cost less than £250, and that the 'cheap' 12/6 faced fierce competition from Austin and Wolseley, both possessed of moderately 'U' images. Understandably, in tax conscious Britain, the smallest Siddeley (still listed, if no longer actually made, in 1936) emerges as top scorer with 11,600 units, followed by the flathead 15 (5500) and its successor, the almost Protean 17 (4260). But the 20, which had to contend with Humber's Snipe and the smaller Buicks, accounted for a respectable 3850 cars in seven seasons, while even the 20/25, which coincided with the first wave of rearmament, sold 884.

Advertised for 'daughters of gentlemen' the Twelve was made in the largest numbers, with over eleven thousand having found buyers by 1936. It could be quite attractive, particularly in drophead form like this Tickford bodied 1933 example with external battery box, photographed still giving good service in the late fifties.

Most of these Siddeleys went to home market customers; curiously, the best overseas outlet was South Africa, where the factory operated a depôt in Durban. A 1933 press release claimed that 'the great majority of the leading doctors, professional men and business magnates' in that city were 'thoroughly satisfied Armstrong Siddeley owners'. Exaggeration? Maybe, but photographs survive of one-make rallies in Natal, and soon afterwards J D Siddeley thought it worth his while to open another branch in Johannesburg. They also cared enough for the export trade to tropicalise the 'finest quality Warwickshire ash' used in body frames.

During our period, of course, everything had six cylinders - the old 14 had disappeared at the end of 1929 - and side by side valves were confined to the

bottom of the range, being phased out during 1935. Flat radiators had gone for good by 1933, wire wheels were usually found only on the more sporting styles, and springs were semi-elliptic all round, exceptions being the cantilevers at the rear of two vintage hangovers, the Special 20 and the Mk II 30. Crankshafts were massive, but seldom ran to more than four mains. The 30, like the Model 34 Marmon that had inspired it, had only three, though this fact was seldom mentioned in factory literature. Only the Siddeley Special ran to seven.

Driver convenience was carefully studied, with three armrests in front, and bench seats on Wilson equipped cars; handbrakes were tucked away on the right to give an unobstructed floor. Windows had a combined slide-and-wind action, anticipating 1934's craze for 'ventipanes'. More commendable still was the sparing use of chromium plate: this was one of 1930's novelties, but it was confined to a narrow strip round the inside of the radiator shell - and to the radiator shutters when these made their appearance late in 1931.

1930's Armstrong Siddeleys were much the same as the 1929s, apart from the chromium plate - and hydraulic dampers. Common to all were magneto ignition, pump circulation assisted by vaned flywheels, and Claudel-Hobson carburettors, a dual choke instrument featuring on the big 30. Clutches were of single plate type, and the three speed gearboxes (with central control) were mounted separately at the front end of the torque tube - a similar location was used for Wilsons when specified. Brakes were cable operated, with four wheel handbrakes on smaller cars, and springs were gaitered. Smallest of the range was the 12/6, a simple four-bearing flathead with the tax dodging dimensions of 56 x 84mm (1236cc). Fuel was fed by gravity from a 6 gallon tank on the dash, and the makers claimed 50-55 mph and 32 mpg. In practice, the 12 wasn't as frugal as that, 24/26 mpg being the norm, but it wasn't impossibly heavy at 2364 lbs, and its 10/30 mph acceleration times - 16 seconds in top, 12 in second - matched those of the heavier family tens, if no match for the Wolseley

Scotland again: a Brunell photograph taken on the 1938 Scottish Rally, showing a Fourteen climbing strongly. Probably a private entry.

Hornet, an elongated Morris Minor and a tight fit for four adults. The price of dignity and first class workmanship was £250 for a tourer, and £285 for a saloon. Both the 12 and the bigger 1.9 litre 15, also a flathead, featured the flat radiator. 15s, however, had an extra nine inches of wheelbase as well as Autovac feed from a rear tank. During the year they would acquire re-designed rear axles, one-shot lubrication, and a four speed Wilson gearbox option which boosted the saloon price from £385 to £425.

Further up the range, the recipe embraced overhead valves, vee radiators, Autovacs and, of course, the Wilson transmission, though the old three speed manual was still nominally available in 1930, if not later. The 2872cc three-bearing 20 came on wheelbases of 120 or 129 inches, with a choice of eight bodies, priced from £425 upwards. Long chassis models had the 30's cantilever rear springs. The 30, on a 135 inch wheelbase, was strictly for chauffeurs at £1450, but though a silver plated carriage with silver upholstery and chromed luggage grid (whatever must JDS have thought?) was commissioned by an Indian lady in 1930, production was down to a trickle: 50 chassis sanctioned that year, and another 20 in 1931. The aged giant would, however, still be quoted in early editions of the '33 catalogue. If commission numbers are any guide, Armstrong Siddeley sold well over 5000 cars in 1930.

Bodies were, of course, their own. Though they would revive the plate of the Burlington Carriage Company (which JDS had taken over in 1913), Burlingtons were 'factory customs' made in the Parkside shops. They were generally restricted to the Siddeley Special range, though a beautiful little 14/6 town car was shown at Olympia in 1936. Sadly, this one (DJJ 14) ended up on the cab rank at Bourne End GWR station in the mid forties. There were also a few catalogued bodies commissioned from familiar names - sundry Tickford dropheads and wind-down convertible saloons were quoted between 1931 and 1934, and 1930 catalogues showed 15 and 20hp fixed head coupés from Grose, not to mention Hoyal's fabric sportsman saloon, also fitted to Buicks, Fiats and Graham-Paiges. The shortcomings of fabric were, however, soon recognised, and it wasn't used after 1931.

Even the smaller Armstrongs contrived to look quite impressive [this is a 1933 Sports saloon on the 20hp chassis] when coachbuilders were kind to them, and whilst built to last were not devoid of urge when endowed with bodywork of reasonable weight.

The main change observed at Olympia in 1930 was a longer stroke, 1434cc engine for the 12/6. During the ensuing year, the car also acquired a three speed preselector option, the 15's back axle, coil ignition, rubber engine and radiator mounts, and a repositioned fuel tank, ahead of the bulkhead instead of behind it. Both 12 and 15 were given new 'turbulent' cylinder heads with centrally located sparking plugs, though at this juncture the story becomes complicated. A new Long 15 (115 ins wheelbase(featured coil ignition, whereas short (111 ins) cars wouldn't receive it until the end of the year. These latter shared the 12's three speed Wilson (Long 15s were four speeders), but both species now had vee radiators. Bigger Armstrong Siddeleys now came with safety glass all round, twin wipers, air cleaners, adjustable steering columns and stop tail lights. Autovacs were giving way to mechanical pumps, and batteries were tucked away under the bonnet, though 12/6s still had battery boxes on their running boards. A fluid flywheel option was available on l.w.b. 20s and 30s: some Short 20s seem to have had this as well.

Bendix brakes made their appearance for 1932, when 20hp engines were given coil ignition and front mounted fans of conventional type, the latter found on 1933 editions of the 15. The new 20 unit was a more powerful 3.2 litre affair with four mains, though to complicate matters there were now two limousine chassis, one to the latest specification and the other (which, surprisingly, cost more) retaining the old engine, magneto ignition, and cantilevers at the rear. Also new on the 20 were the thermostatically controlled radiator shutters: these allowed some economies, since a flat core could be concealed behind a convincing looking vee. The Sphinx sat down (in protest?) and there was a move towards tidier facias with circular dials, though rectangular instruments persisted for the time price Economy 12/6 had an oval grouping all too reminiscent of a Morris Oxford. This one was a real bargain at £260: it was also the only flat radiator model in the 1932 catalogue. Announced with a three speed Wilson, it (and the Short 15) had been given an extra forward ratio by February 1932.

Bodies were modified, the latest 20s featuring an inswept tail panel which not only covered the dumb irons and fuel tank but also incorporated a tiny luggage locker on the lines of the traditional coachmaker's 'boodge'. This shape would remain as the classic

six light Siddeley for the rest of our period. The companion sports saloon derived from a one-off made for A-S sales director H P Henry in 1930: it was of four light configuration with thin pillars and projecting boot. Too angular to be acceptable in the ensuing 'streamline' craze, it survived for only three seasons, though not before it had been adapted to the 12 and 15hp chassis as well. Even more attractive was a 'Rally Tourer' available on Short 20s and Long 15s. The rally commemorated was the first of the RAC marathons, incidentally, and not the Alpine, which had seen a works entry from Parkside.

Rallying as such was no novelty. S C H Davis had taken a Short 20 saloon through the 1931 Monte as a test of the Wilson gearbox, and shortly afterwards the company published his glowing testimonial (*The Silver Sphinx Goes South*). With a mere 2.9 litres under the bonnet, the flywheel apparently took kindly to 'instantaneous changes', and Davis was rewarded with the *Concours de Confort*, still very much on the agenda, and a British preserve - Wolseleys would win it in 1936, 1937 and 1939. W F Bradley, *The Autocar*'s Continental correspondent, drove a similar car in the '31 Alpine, making third best British performance - behind an Invicta and a Roesch Talbot.

Beaten only by Aldington's 2 litre BMW in the Torquay Rally, this pretty Sports Foursome coupé on the short chassis Seventeen is seen here entered for the 1936 Coachwork competition. Ingles, a Scot who had previously been with Argyll, and who was first and only manager of A-S's own coachbuilders, Burlington, saved 1 cwt on this body, by use of aluminium alloys. Boasting vermilion upholstery and fitted with high compression pistons, the car was driven by Douglas Scott [on the right, wearing a cap] and the young man on his right, who later became chairman of Lodge Plugs.

Thus Siddeley were encouraged to field a team of four Short 20s in 1932, their rakish, American style roadster bodies looking incongruous behind the dignified vee radiators. Once again Bradley drove, his team mates being Cyril Siddeley (later the second Lord Kenilworth), Humfrey Symons, and Antonio Lago, by now peddling Wilsons round Europe. (He was, of course, his own best customer at Automobiles Talbot, but some boxes were sold to Delahaye and Isotta Fraschini.) Cyril Siddeley, incidentally, considered Lago a 'second rate driver', and he spoilt Armstrong Siddeley's chances of a team award by losing four points, though the others collected Glacier Cups. This was the works' last Alpine, though they made a mass onslaught on the '34 RAC event with the Rainbow Team of Sports 12s, finished in all the colours of the spectrum. (A contemporary experiment - cramming every shade from violet to yellow onto three such cars - was reported in *The Autocar* - but sounds like a leg-pull.) One of the Alpine 20s survives to this day in Wiltshire.

The 1933-4 period saw the consolidation of all the recent improvements, with one-shot lubrication standardised throughout the range, along with rear tanks on 12s and some additions to the extras list, notably DWS permanent jacks and trafficators. The Economy 12 - not quoted after 1933 - was given a slight vee to its grille, while 15hp engines were enlarged to 2.2 litres, the long chassis version resembling a scaled down 20 with identical coachwork. The 20 itself was now made only in 3.2 litre form with a downdraught carburettor, this latter featuring on 1934 editions of the side valve cars. Two seaters had been discontinued, but tourers were still available on the 12, 15 and Short 20. But the major news was a sensational luxury car unveiled at Olympia in October 1932 - a long overdue replacement for the 30.

This, like its predecessor, was an ohv six of 5 litre capacity, with the current Bendix brakes and four speed Wilson box. Here, however, all resemblance to past designs ceased. The Siddeley Special wasn't - initially, at any rate - aimed at the stately carriage market - the 12ft wheelbase option came later. Nor could one really call it competition, for the as yet unborn Derby Bentley and M45 Lagonda. Rather was it JDS' own conception of a super-car, executed by Fred Allard, a draughtsman who came from Swift and who worked on the engine, and Ernest Siddeley.

To the traditional 'aircraft quality' had been added aircraft techniques. The new wet liner engine broke with tradition in having a seven bearing crankshaft, but more important was the use of hiduminium alloy for block, head, crankcase, sump, pistons and connecting rods. Shared with lesser Siddeleys were the frontal fan, downdraught carburettor (later cars had twin horizontal SUs) and mechanical pump feed, though the Special boasted a supplementary electric system as well. The double drop frame of 132 ins wheelbase rode on semi-elliptic springs. For all those fancy alloys, the car was no lightweight. Even Vanden Plas' handsome sports tourer turned the scales at 4256 lbs, and short saloons weighed in at close on 2¼ tons. On this one the fluid flywheel was a desirable extra (you couldn't swap cogs fast with the standard box), though 1935's Mk II Special pioneered the centrifugal clutch later fitted to regular Armstrong Siddeleys. Also found on Mk IIs were hydraulic valve lifters, a longer chassis with the engine set further forward and rear seats within the wheelbase, and some necessary vacuum-servo assistance for the brakes.

Short chassis Specials were good for

Fairly or no, the marque has always laboured under a rather stuffy image, and this 1938 Seventeen is more in keeping with the popular idea of a medium sized car from the range. Bodied by Salmons, originally as a saloon, this example was later returned to the coach-builders for conversion into a landaulette, as illustrated.

Echoing the thrusting and rather aggressive vee radiator of its twenties predecessors, this Twenty photographed in Worth Forest in March 1931 was in direct competition with Humber's Snipe and the smaller Buicks, but nevertheless managed 3850 units in seven seasons. Most bodies were built in the factory or by Charlesworth, although some of the earlier ones favoured Connaught.

the ton, which ensured a genuine 60 mph (about the norm for a family 12), but the most the little car could sustain on a 5.33 top gear was 55. Not that this mattered in tennis and bridge circles. The coupé was quiet, comfortable and flexible, and it cost only £285, less than a Riley 9 and the same as Triumph's Gloria. 600 Sports 12s found buyers in two seasons.

Flatheads were nevertheless on their way out, and for the third year in succession Siddeley had something new for the '34 Show, the 2394cc 17. This can be regarded as scaled down 20 or uprated ohv 15; prices included bumpers and permanent jacks even if the 'thermostatic' shutters were no longer functional. Further, the 17 was all things to all men. Rather than espouse the all too familiar formula of big chassis/small engine, the company offered their new model in three wheelbases - 111 ins for the owner driver, 116 ins for the family man, and 123½ ins for those who wanted a compact town carriage. Most attractive of the bunch, and good for 70 mph, was the Sports Foursome on the short chassis, a scaled up 12 coupé with projecting boot, though there was still a tourer in the 'medium' range. By the end of 1935, 17s (and 20s as well) had been given the Special's new centrifugal clutch, which saved band wear more than somewhat.

With the 15 out of the way, the 12 was next on the list for relegation, speeded out of production by 1935's tax concessions. Pint sized sixes were not only out of fashion: they were no longer economic necessities. It is significant that the 12's replacement, initially sold as the 12 Plus, had become a 14 by 1937 in recognition of changing tastes. (In export markets, incidentally, it carried a 14/45 label which must have delighted M Roesch!)

This wasn't entirely coincidence. The Siddeley's cylinder dimensions were identical to the Talbot's, at 61 x 95mm (1666cc). The first 12 Plus cars (which included the last Armstrong Siddeley tourers) used the 12's 105 ins wheelbase and perpendicular saloon bodywork, but early in the model's career the chassis was lengthened by three inches and given a new body with slanting screen and

85-90 mph, cruised quietly in the 70s, and took 14 seconds to reach 60 through the gears. As well as the catalogued Burlingtons - a classic sports saloon and a long chassis limousine - there were sedancas from Thrupp and Maberly and Lancefield, an elegant two door VDP coupé de ville, and a strange slab sided two door sports saloon with pontoon wings, commissioned from Lancefield by George Wansbrough and entered by him in the 1934 RAC Rally. Sir Malcolm Campbell bought one of the first saloons, and a tourer was supplied to the Crown Prince of Denmark in 1933. Though sales of 235 units were creditable for so large and expensive a vehicle - Mk I saloons cost £995, raised to £1050 with the advent of Mk II - the Special was phased out during 1937.

Hot on the heels of this Grand Tourer came something sporty for the distaff side, the 'girls' coupé first seen at Olympia in 1933. 'An ideal possession,' rhapsodised Parkside, 'known everywhere for its Pace with Grace'.

It was certainly pretty. A shorter than standard 97 inch wheelbase was used, and wire wheels were regular equipment on both coupés and the companion sports tourers which took their bow in the famous Rainbow Team. The absence of side pillars suggested a parallel with the Humber Vogue, but the Siddeley's simple fastback was less ponderous than Rootes' French style top opening trunk, and as usual there wasn't an inch of superfluous chromium plate in sight. Performance, alas! just wasn't there. Weight was down to just over

It has been said that John Davenport Siddeley had strong ideas on how his cars should be driven, and certainly the company encouraged owners to care for their cars consicentiously. Not only does this come through in the exhortations of the instruction book and workshop manual, but in items like this calendar for 1930 upon which chauffeurs and owner drivers could meticulously record their mileage. Clearly the model for which the calendar has been used must date from the previous decade, but the last recorded figure of 92,784 miles gives a good indication of the marque's staying power.

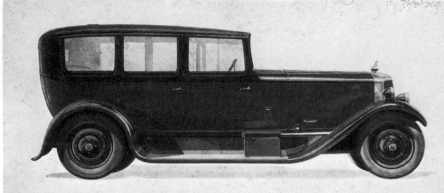

Armstrong Siddeley
CALENDAR AND MILEAGE RECORD FOR 1930

Week ending	Speedometer Reading		Week ending	Speedometer Reading		Week ending	Speedometer Reading		Week ending	Speedometer Reading	
	Total	Week		Total	Week		Total	Week		Total	Week
Jan. 2	84,853	207	April 2	86,806	93	July 2	90,701	285	Oct. 1		
9	84,269	216	Summer Time starts 9	86,961	155	9	90,931	230	Summer Time ends 8		
16	84,526	257	Easter 16	87,240	279	16	91,322	391	15		
23	84,879	353	23	87,594	354	23	91,553	231	22		
Feb 30	85,126	247	May 30	87,711	117	30	91,727	174	Nov 29		
Feb 6	85,289	163	May 7	88,006	295	Aug 6	91,803	76	Nov 5		
13	85,446	157	14	88,421	415	13	92,195	392	12		
20	85,801	355	21	88,598	177	20	92,575	380	19		
Mar 27	85,976	175	28	88,713	115	27	92,784	209	26		
Mar 5	86,051	75	June 4	88,970	257	Sept. 3			Dec. 3		
12	86,179	128	11	89,381	411	10			10		
19	86,363	184	18	89,976	595	17			17		
26 Renew Licence	86,713	350	25 Renew Licence	90,416	440	24 Renew Licence			Christmas 24 Renew Licence		
Total for Quarter	2660		Total for Quarter	3703		Total for Quarter			Total for Quarter		

Armstrong Siddeley Motors Ltd., Coventry
10, OLD BOND STREET, LONDON, W.1. & 35, KING STREET WEST, MANCHESTER

sloping tail panel. At 2800 lbs the 14 wasn't much heavier than the last 12s, and its 65 mph and 24 mpg were entirely adequate for its public. At £320 it contributed another 3750 units to the score, and was still listed in 1939.

If sporting themes were on their way out - the Sports Foursome 17 wasn't quoted after 1936 - the body department wasn't short on good ideas. The Touring Saloon, first seen on the 'medium' 17 in 1936 (it was later applied to the 14 and 20/25 as well) was just what its name implied - a roomy six light affair with a big external access boot and folding tables built into the back of the bench front seat. Very handsome was the Atalanta, the last of the pre-war Sports saloons, and usually sold with wire wheels. This one was reserved for the two bigger chassis, though something very similar was offered on 1937 and 1938 14s. Finally, there was the perpendicular Town and Country, for those who employed a chauffeur but sometimes liked to drive themselves; it was a Coach Saloon with a fully disappearing division, offered, like the Atalanta, on the 17 and 20/25.

By now instruments were grouped neatly in twin dials, and in the summer of 1936 the 20 at long last gave way to the 20/25, in two wheelbase lengths; the bigger 3.7 litre power unit, however, added another 3½ ins to the short chassis. The rest of it was copybook Siddeley, even if a horizontal SU replaced the traditional Claudel-Hobson carburettor. This long standing connection was to be broken for good in 1938, probably because Hobsons were now fully committed to the aircraft industry. Output was 85 bhp at 3600 rpm, and the rest of the specification reflected standard practice - centrifugal clutch, one-shot lubrication, and Bendix brakes. On a 4.09 axle ratio saloons were capable of 75-80 mph, while the heavy limousine would cruise in the low 70s on a 4.7 top gear. Among those who chose this stately carriage (it competed with the Humber Pullman at £745) were Neville Chamberlain, who bought his second car of the type in May 1939, and the Crown Prince of Denmark, who preferred a locally built body not unlike the Touring Saloon in shape. Other Royal owners (Prince Arthur of Connaught, King Carol of Rumania) opted for the Long 17, while Armstrong Siddeley's H P Henry had a

short chassis 20/25 with razor edge touring limousine coachwork by Mayfair. This led to speculation as to factory built coachwork in this idiom, but though vestiges of a new trend were apparent in the 16 of 1939, the full treatment wouldn't be applied until 1949's four light Whitley.

14s and 17s continued without significant change, though the latest Short 17 saloon was something of a bargain at £395. Body was essentially the 14's, but equipment included the usual three armrests, a rug in the back, and a reserve fuel supply.

1938's big news was, of course, 'balanced drive', the company's solution to the problem of separate rubber mounts for engine and gearbox. Logically enough, they adopted unit construction: at the same time, steering ratios were raised, and horizontal bonnet louvres made their appearance. Chassis and bodies were otherwise as before: the 14, the two longer 17s and the 20/25 would continue into 1939 with no alterations beyond the addition of radio to the official extras list.

The cost accountants were, however, at work, and the result could be seen at Earls Court in 1938 - an all new 2 litre 16 with the classic dimensions of 65 x 100mm. Chassis weight was saved by making the floor pan integral with the frame in the manner of 1939's new Austins, but there were other less pleasing signs of a tight budget; a horrible umbrella-handle handbrake, instruments that wouldn't have looked out of place on a Hillman, and a snap-up Sphinx which doubled as filler cap instead of a proper screwdown affair. One still, however, got one-shot lubrication and permanent jacks (Jackalls this time), and tools were housed in a neat pull-out drawer under the dash. For the £398 customers received an updated edition of the traditional Coach Saloon with a bigger projecting boot. A four light Sports type was available at the same price.

Mechanically, there were few dramatic changes, though the carburettor was a Zenith, dampers were of piston type, and the rod operated Girling brakes were more

predictable than the old Bendix. Gear ratios - 5.1, 7.24, 10.67 and 18.4 to 1 - were not exactly sporting, and the foursquare 16 rolled somewhat if pressed to the limit through a corner, but weight was down to 3024 lbs, and the car cruised happily at 55-60 mph. In traffic, the high driving position made it a pleasanter mount than later Lancasters and Hurricanes, on which bonnets *appeared* to slope uphill! An unexplained gimmick on at least two pre-war 17s I've encountered was a leather jacket over the rocker cover, presumably to cut down on the decibels.

In the alarmist, post-Munich climate, sales of 950 units in a twelve-month compare favourably with the 5045 cars made between 1945 and 1948. In any case, the 16 fared better than its companion, the New Twenty, which got no further than the last pre-war Show. Even factory records are unhelpful, though the ASOC's Mike Godfrey opines that a batch of six mysterious 25hp cars (not part of the regular 20/25 sequence) represents the sum total of production.

In most respects this last 20 was a crossbred 16/17 on a 120 ins wheelbase, with a capacity of 2.8 litres (75 x 105mm). Bodies were inherited from the 17 - a restyled Coach Saloon, the Atalanta, and the Town and Country. There were, however, three significant differences: a heater was standard, there was ride control for the Luvax dampers, and at long last i.f.s. had reached Parkside in the form of an André Girling coil set-up. Prices followed the old 20hp pattern, starting at £535. It's tempting to assume that the new suspension was at fault, especially in view of the torsion bars adopted in 1945, but one wonders why. After all, the selfsame system worked admirably on smaller Daimlers and Lanchesters, and wasn't discarded until 1953.

As members of the Hawker Siddeley Consortium, Armstrong Siddeley Motors were immediately engulfed by war work, and no 1940 models were even announced. However, the prompt appearance of the new 16s in 1945 suggests that their mechanical specification, if not their styling, must

have been finalised before the war. Certainly they were winners from the start, for all their heretical looks: I remember my first encounter with a Hurricane late in 1945, and wondering what on earth the Sphinx was doing on something that couldn't conceivably be an Armstrong Siddeley!

Nonetheless, those 16s (and the later 18s) retained a lot of the old charm, especially the Typhoon. This must surely rate as the world's first series production hardtop, a good 2½ years ahead of Buick's much publicised Riviera. The cars drove like Siddeleys, too; even if the synchromesh box felt out of place, you could still have a Wilson. But they were just a little too flashy for country solicitors, doctors and their ladies - and this isn't just the opinion of one elderly diehard. In 1948, Hawker Siddeley's H K Jones was touring South Africa in a Typhoon. Here he encountered a 1935 car and its devoted owner. This gentleman had but one word for the latest fashion in hardtops ... 'Retrograde'.

If only he'd waited for a Sapphire ...

THE SPECIALISTS

It wasn't so very long ago, back in the fifties, when it looked as though a few more years
would see the complete disappearance of all the traditional crafts
associated with the manufacture of motorcars of the veteran and vintage era.
One by one, the old respected coachbuilding firms
closed their doors or turned to other, more profitable, activities
and the ranks of the Institute of British Carriage and Automobile Manufacturers
[IBCAM] were drawn increasingly from the commercial vehicle world
and from the design offices of the mass producers. Similarly, old established
garage businesses, many of them dating back to the days of the village smithy
and the horse and carriage, became absorbed into large conglomerates
and multi-national chains.

The Editor's 1921 Angus-Sanderson with partly completed ash body framing made by Bob Gill. Bob also made the locks, door hinges, hood irons, luggage grid and spare wheel carrier [not shown]. The bodywork was copied faithfully from the only other A-S running in Britain.

RATIONALISATION became the order of the day, and there was a grave danger that before long early motor cars would be forced off the road for lack of spares, tyres and the specialised services upon which their owners so often depended. Happily, however, this did not happen and almost at the eleventh hour (for many of the older craftsmen were of advanced years and there would be no one to pass on the skills to the new generation) there came an upsurge of interest in early cars. Possibly due in some measure to the popularity of the film *Genevieve* and fostered by the Veteran Car Club of Great Britain, the Vintage Sports Car Club and progressive one-make clubs like the Bullnosed Morris Club and Humber Register, this interest continued and has never been higher than it is today.

Because of the demand, and the passage of time, fewer early cars are now found in useable condition each year and it is perhaps fortunate for the continuing health of the vintage and veteran movement that enthusiasm,

particularly in Great Britain, should be at such a level as to make it worthwhile for a whole army of specialists to cater for the needs of enthusiasts today.

Before it was too late, the secrets of composite body construction were passed on, small engineering firms now exist who can (and will) make virtually any component for any make of early car, and vehicles which twenty years ago would have been considered beyond restoration now occupy the attentions of these specialists. The result is that, in 1979, a large number of newly restored cars are still being brought out for their first 'airing' long after the time when, so sceptics predicted, the supply would have 'dried up'.

For all this, we have the specialists to thank, and whilst obviously we can mention only a few in these pages, we would like to pay tribute to all those firms who, whether devoted solely to early vehicle work or not, have contributed - indeed, are still contributing - so handsomely to the hobby

which we all enjoy.

MARSH DEVELOPMENTS

Mike Marsh is an airline pilot with a passion for cars. Back in 1975 he started to gather together a team of men whose lives had been spent in the coachbuilding trade to concentrate on the production of wings and running boards and other body parts for early Morris and MG cars.

From these early days in Guildford, however, the company quickly expanded and is now located at Bolney Grange Industrial Estate, Hickstead, although it is fast outgrowing the accommodation available there as well. This expansion is the direct result of increasing demand for one-off bodywork for all makes of car, and complete body construction now accounts for all work undertaken.

Some indication of the versatility of

the Marsh craftsmen may be gained by an examination of the list of vehicles which have passed through the shop in recent months. Included among these are a Type 57 Bugatti (new front wings), Bugatti Atlantique (accident damage to complete body shell), Model K 1925 Cubitt (front and rear wings and running boards), Malallieu Bentley (aluminium bonnet), MG PA Type (complete new body) and a brace of 1934.

What is also encouraging is that the workforce now includes a number of young skilled craftsmen, ensuring that the traditions are carried on and passed to a new generation when the time comes.

Not only do the company reproduce existing designs either. They can, if required, design and build a complete motor body, and are at the moment working on the prototype of a large sports racing car. Modern designs frequently call for light steel frames rather than the traditional ash, and this work is also carried out.

Whilst trimming, painting and mechanical work are at present sent to outside specialists, these will eventually become 'in house' activities and in the meantime the company incorporates skills as delicate as those of the locksmith with those as robust as the blacksmith with panel-beating in steel and aluminium.

Current projects include a complete new bodyshell for a Ferrari racing car, a new body for a Phantom I Rolls-Royce, rear bodywork for Lanchester and Armstrong-Siddeley - the former a drophead coupé by Ranelagh and the latter a four door saloon with factory body, and a complete body and wings for the Editor's 1921 Angus-Sanderson 14hp tourer. The accompanying illustrations will give some indication of the standard of work carried out.

MARSTON RADIATORS

When Serck withdrew from vintage radiator restoration the prospect could have been bleak for enthusiasts, since early motorcars - like early houses - tend to suffer with their plumbing in old age. Well, don't we all?

Although Marstons have been running their Vintage Radiator Restoration Unit at Canley for just five

The *Blue Peter* vintage 1928 Humber 14/40 radiator being restored in the workshop of Marston Radiator Services' Vintage Radiator Restoration Unit.

years, they need no real introduction to owners of early cars since they have been involved with the building and repairing of radiators since the early 1900's when John Marston's company marketed the first Sunbeam car, but in fact a prototype car was built in 1899 and the whole of this - including the radiator - was built in the Marston works.

During their long history, Marstons have built radiators for Rolls-Royce, Wolseley, Vauxhall, Albion, Beardmore and Austin, and, significantly, for Sir Henry Segrave's record-breaking Sunbeam which achieved 203.7928 mph at Daytona Beach on Tuesday, 29th March 1926. Derek Warner, who runs the Canley restoration unit, however, is not one to rest on past laurels, and whilst there are other firms offering restoration services at a lower price no compromises whatsoever are made in standards of workmanship or quality of materials.

Not only do the company repair and build from scratch radiators for every possible make of veteran and vintage car, commercial, or even aeroplane, they also undertake the fabrication of stone guards, fuel and oil tanks, small radiators for water-cooled motorcycles, bumpers and other brightwork. They can also supply any type of matrix and many marque badges. In addition to this restoration activity, the company's main income is, of course, derived from the manufacture and repair and servicing of radiators for every type of modern car from a string of branches nationwide.

COLDWELL ENGINEERING

It's no good having the most beautiful bodywork ever created if the chassis of the car is in poor condition and it is fortunate, therefore, that the revival of traditional coachbuilding

John Cockayne, the proprietor, working on the Sheffield-Simplex chassis. Note the massive engine bearers acting as chassis cross-members.

has been accompanied by the establishing of an increasing number of specialist workshops catering for all types of mechanical overhaul, repair and restoration.

John Cockayne's Coldwell Engineering in Sheffield is just one of many where the enthusiast can be assured of the right attention regardless of the obscurity of the marque concerned, but particularly if the patient happens to be a Rolls-Royce Silver Ghost or Phantom I.

John's interest in early motorcars dates back to 1954 when he purchased a 1926 3 litre Bentley (which he still owns) for £220. Those were the days!

He stripped this car down to the bare chassis and rebuilt it, but it was to be another twenty years before he was able to concentrate his energies on mechanical engineering.

In 1974, the family business, of which he was both director and accountant, was sold and at last he was able to seek an outlet for his long-standing interest in mechanical things in general and vintage cars in particular.

Late in 1974, and having worked at home for six months restoring a Silver Ghost, he purchased Coldwell Engineering, took on an experienced assistant, and decided to concentrate on early models of Rolls-Royce - particularly Ghosts and Phantom Is.

In the past five years the business has grown, as has the staff and the

Work currently in hand includes: Lea-Francis Sports (complete chassis rebuild), Rolls 20/25 (minor chassis repairs and engine rebuild), two Phantom Is (chassis repairs and engine rebuild), Silver Ghost (new gears for gearbox), Silver Ghost (engine rebuild) and, interestingly, a 1909 Type LA 2 45hp Sheffield-Simplex which merits more than a mere mention.

There are three Sheffield-Simplexes known to survive: one is in the Sydney Museum in Australia (we assume that this is the 1912 example which used to be owned by the New South Wales Technical Museum and which was stored in an old wool warehouse at Kensington, Australia, near the old British Leyland works); one ex-Earl Fitzwilliam (the postwar 1921 7.7 litre double Victoria originally kept in Ireland, exported to America, recently re-imported by Coys of Kensington and at the time of writing on offer by Trojan Ltd for a reputed £30,000 - the City of Sheffield didn't want to know!) and the car in John Cockayne's care.

Minus bodywork, the chassis is almost complete but for the torque tube and back axle (which incorporates the two speed gearbox and brakes, etc) which, so legend has it, now repose at the bottom of an Australian swamp. The original rear hubs and wheel are, however, intact.

Despite extensive advertising and, not surprisingly, the missing components have not been located, but comprehensive research has provided Coldwell Engineering with sufficient detailed data to make possible production of accurate replica components. Design of these missing parts is in progress and is proving very interesting. Normally, of course, specifications required in restoration work are known or can be obtained from existing components. In this case, however, they are having to be worked out from basic principles - eg, poundage of valve springs, gear proportion and ratios, stress calculations, etc. This is a most worthwhile restoration project, which follows the re-importation of the vehicle from Australia (coincidentally) and Coldwell Engineering are to be congratulated upon tackling such an exacting task.

In future issues of the Vintage Car Annual we shall be looking at other specialists in the field. If readers have favourable experience of specific firms or individuals then we will, of course, be pleased to include them upon receiving details.

accumulated detailed working knowledge of these cars. Special tools and jigs have been developed, all the available technical data has been amassed, and the firm's small machine shop is able to produce simple components which cannot be obtained elsewhere.

They are now in a position to supply new replacement parts produced for Silver Ghost and Phantom I and are able to meet the demand for virtually all the spare parts normally required in an engine rebuild 'off the shelf'.

In this, John is fortunate in the location of the works, since Sheffield is an ideal centre for this type of work and almost every service is available within a few miles radius of his workshops. These include forging, casting, supply of alloy steels, heat treatment, machining, metal spraying, spark erosion, electro-plating and stove enamelling.

Coldwell Engineering are also equipped to carry out repairs and servicing for regular customers and also offer a reconditioning service for assemblies such as carburettors, shock absorbers, universal joints, etc. Whilst last year about 40% of their business involved European customers, they more usually cater for those resident in the Midlands or North of England and can also offer engine rebuilds - the completed units being tested on a testing rig.

Whilst concentrating on mechanical work. the company can turn their hands to minor accident repair work but usually coordinate and supervise coachwork by outside specialists.

DOUGLAS

**It is often forgotten that many of the major motorcycle firms have, from time to time, essayed car production with varying degrees of success.
Among these one can include Matchless, Ariel, Clyno and AJS
[Humber, Rover, Lea-Francis and Sunbeam being, on the contrary, car firms who also built motorcycles] - the most notable success being Triumph.
Here, V C CHAMBERLAIN looks at one of the more promising designs to emerge during the cyclecar era immediately before the Great War.**

IN 1913 Douglas Brothers of Kingswood, Bristol, were well known for their 2¾ hp horizontal twin motorcycle, which won the TT that year, an event which was just the beginning of an astonishing run of successes in that field. Few persons today, however, remember or have even heard of the Douglas car, which was launched the same year.

This is hardly surprising, since, in all, very few of them were produced and hardly any, if indeed any at all, have survived. (*Maybe one. -Ed*) At the time, however, the car was well received and had some successes in

sporting events. The key to this car development on the part of a firm manufacturing motorcycles was the Williamson engine.

In 1912 the firm became closely associated with the Coventry motorcycle firm of Williamson, who were interested in the heavier type of motorcycle.

Actually, Mr Williamson was related, by marriage, to the Douglas family and it was natural that he should turn to them for the manufacture of a large horizontal-twin engine. As a result, a Williamson shop was opened, producing an 8hp 1070cc

engine, both air-cooled and water-cooled.

With light cars becoming popular, it was almost inevitable that someone at Douglas's should think of designing and manufacturing a light car since the horizontal twin was extremely smooth running and had many of the attributes of a four cylinder engine, which was the more usual in a car.

The brains behind the Douglas car project was probably Willie Douglas, the popular son of the founder of the

Miss Addis-Price at Brooklands in her Douglas Special in 1922.

It is difficult to say just how many cars were produced, but it is interesting to note that the firm commenced negotations for the purchase of a factory site at Yate for car production. With the outbreak of war, however, the firm concentrated its production on motorcycles, generating sets and other products for the war effort. After the war, car production resumed with renewed energy. Manufacture of the Williamson engine ceased, permitting the Light Car Department to move into the Williamson shop and a new, much improved and larger 1224cc engine of 10.5hp, with self-starter, was introduced.

Several models were made available, including a new four-seater, with four speeds, but by this time post-war inflation had doubled the price.

Rigorous tests proved very favourable and several leading persons in the motoring and sporting world turned to the Douglas, and among these was John Alcock, the well-known aviator, who supplemented his Humber with a saloon version, said to be the only one made.

As one might expect, members of the Douglas firm supported their own product and Les Bailey, the racing motorcyclist, who was now works manager, had a two-seater; head of the firm, William Douglas, Senior, had a particularly fine coupé built for his own use and for many years, long after production had ceased, he travelled to work in this car, chauffeur driven by Johnson and leaving his Rolls at home!

Willie Douglas favoured a standard tourer, and it was said that he once turned it over on his way to Weston-Super-Mare, and was rescued by a troop of soldiers!

On the sporting front the new Douglas car had some successes and a special overhead-valve engine was produced for speed events. Billy Gibbs won the Lester Cup in the 1920 London to Land's End Trial and two gold medals in the London to Edinburgh Run of the same year, whilst in 1920 a Douglas was successful at Brooklands, achieving sixty-six miles per hour; and it was also at Brooklands, in 1922, that Miss Addis-Price won the Essex Junior Short Handicap in a Douglas Special, but in spite of all these high recommendations and successes, it seems that few cars were sold after the war. Competition from firms specialising in four wheeled vehicles, and using the latest mass-production methods, proved too fierce and it was the Douglas motorcycle which was to prove so successful throughout the twenties and to occupy all the resources of the company. A half-hearted revival in 1932 during the Depression, and featuring a 750cc engine and cantilever springing, scarcely left the drawing board and the firm wisely stuck to two wheels to see them through this difficult period.

firm, although Williamson themselves essayed a three-wheeled chain driven cyclecar in 1913.

A Light Car Department was opened in 1912 under Bert Howes and before long prototypes were to be seen in the streets of Bristol and Bath. They varied in detail, common features being the Williamson engine, friction disc transmission, and worm drive to the rear axle, and by the end of 1913 a model was offered to the public at £160.

The engine, a modified Williamson, was mounted transversely across the chassis, the casing of the three speed gearbox, with reverse, was cast integrally with the crankcase and the pressed steel frame was upswept at the rear. The clutch was of the leather to metal type, some ten inches in diameter, with final drive by means of a propeller shaft, and bevels to the live rear axle.

Riley detachable wheels were specified, with an efficient braking system at the rear and coil rear springs. The radiator had a vee profile with the starting handle protruding through the centre in a convenient position, and coachwork took the form of metal panelling on an ash framework.

The general effect was that of a two seater coupé with a cabriolet hood,

fitted with irons, so that it could be raised or lowered.

A narrow bodied sports model was also listed, without hood, finish being of a high standard, in either Bristol Red or Medium Green, with black leather button type upholstery, which set off the colours to advantage.

Internally there was a wooden dashboard, with equipment including a sight feed for the oil supply, switch gear for the electric lights, a speedometer in brass, and a Klaxon horn, whilst the wood rim steering wheel was fitted with a hand throttle and advance/retard levers, also in brass, operated from the top of the steering column. The gear lever and handbrake were both fitted on the right.

A *Cyclecar* reporter was given a trial run in one of the first production models and 'all-on' over fifty miles per hour was recorded on a level stretch of road in Bristol, and the car climbed the long hill up to Kingswood - about one in ten - without falling below 25 mph. As with the motorcycle, a strenuous testing programme was insisted upon, Billy Gibbs driving one of the sports cars in the 1913 Six Days Trial, held over a tough course in the Pennines, and winning a gold medal. Willie Douglas himself also had some success on the sands at Weston-Super-Mare.

FN
KING OF THE BELGIANS

Despite its small size, the contribution which Belgium made to automobile design and development generally can only be regarded in retrospect as impressive. More than sixty makes of car, including such revered makes as Germain, Minerva, Excelsior, Imperia and Pipe, all first saw the light of day here, and the standard of engineering overall was always extremely high. It was Belgian refugees whose expertise made possible the tremendous output of shells and munitions in Britain during the First War; Camille Jenatzy, the first man to reach a speed of more than 65 mph in his electric *La Jamais Contente* in 1899 was Belgian; one of the fathers of the modern motor industry, Emile Levassor, was also from the Low Countries; and no less impressive was the rôle played by the Fabrique Nationale d'Armes de Guerre in Belgian automobile history. Better known as FN, and with their products still well known all over the world, they are here examined by HANS KUIPERS and due credit is given for their contribution.

The earliest production FN which appeared in 1900 offered wheel steering, a two speed gearbox and belt-cum-chain drive. Prototypes utilised air cooling for the twin cylinder engine, but water cooling was adopted for production models. A successful model, the car collected three first prizes at the Paris World Fair.

This 1905 rear entrance tonneau follows conventional Continental lines with tubular chassis, full elliptic springing all round and non-detachable wheels. A conventional system of pedal controls [the earlier models relied on a foot pedal reverse] is allied to shaft drive although gears are still changed by the lever on the steering column.

The 1908 '1400' adopted a conventional change speed lever, albeit this, like the hand brake, is located outside the body. Whether or not the unusual demountable windscreen was offered as standard is not known. The Belgian-made Engelbert tyres are still reliant upon security bolts to hold them firmly in place.

This 10CV model dates from 1909 and sports a full four seater side entrance tonneau body. Once again the unusual detachable windscreen is employed and the driver is poised, with hand on the bulb, to sound the horn at any unwary pedestrian.

FABRIQUE Nationale d'Armes de Guerre was founded in 1889 by a group of gunsmiths to manufacture an order from the Belgian Government for 150,000 Mauser infantry rifles. To meet the delivery requirements for an order of this importance, a new factory was established to mass produce these weapons in the most efficient and economical way. The enterprise was a success and well before deliveries had been completed, the company decided both to carry on with the production of military weapons and to manufacture the ammunition they required. In this they were encouraged by orders coming from various governments. The optimism engendered by this success was, nevertheless, moderated by existing competition in this field, and the management decided to ensure the future of their enterprise by widening their activities. To this end, quantity production of components for sporting weapons and 50,000 calibre .22 sporting rifles was undertaken.

FN signed their first contract with the American inventor John M Browning in July 1897 - a memorable date in the history of the company. This was a licence to manufacture his automatic pistol calibre 7.65mm. Many others followed and all over the world the prestige of the name of Browning, linked to an automatic weapon manufactured by FN signified quality.

To diversify their products and to compensate for variations in supply and demand, FN developed many alternative lines of manufacture, some of which have not thrived in comparison with the production of weapons and ammunition, whilst others have known, or still enjoy, a considerable importance in the company's affairs.

This large limousine on the 2400 chassis dates from 1911 and superseded the 1600. A four cylinder car with disc type metal to metal clutch, this model features very long rear springs, rear mounted petrol tank. The box on the roof is not to accommodate Madame's hats, but houses the spare wheel

Of these, the motor driven vehicle is the most noteworthy and, in latter years, the jet engine, which has played an important part in the company's turnover for about fifteen years. Other products manufactured at present are artillery and Hawk guided missiles, airborne vehicles and dairy equipment, knitting machines, motor cycles, mopeds and gas turbines for installation in tanks.

Taken on the whole, FN's activities have continually developed, although twice interrupted by periods of more than four years during the World Wars, from 1914 to 1918 and from 1939 to 1945, and in spite of considerable damage inflicted during the bombardments of the Second War.

At the present time, FN employs about 12,000 persons and 9500 machine tools are in use. The author-

ised capital is 630,000,000 Belgian Francs. The main factory is in Herstal, but the enterprise also possesses industrial plant in Bruges, Ghent (textile machines), Zutendael, Liers and Pontisse. In all, these cover an area of 100 hectares, of which 57 are covered by industrial buildings.

Like many other prominent arms manufacturers, FN took an early interest in the newly invented motor car, and as early as 1900 took the decision to produce their own. Understandably, it followed the pattern of most other pioneer makes, boasted a two cylinder engine, two speed gearbox, belt primary drive and chain final drive, but eschewed tiller steering in favour of a steering wheel, being one of the first companies to adopt this as standard. The engine was of the watercooled, side valve type (an air-cooled version was not proceeded with) and gear changing relied upon a lever on the steering wheel providing two speeds, whilst a foot pedal gave reverse. This first car was well received, gaining three first prizes at the World Fair in Paris.

Shortly following its introduction, this first model was modified considerably and the range was extended, two models now being available: the Model A called *Mignonette à Deux Places* and the Model D. Many types of coachwork were available, including Duc, the tonneau, which could seat four persons, the Victoria and the Rothschild and finally the Jardiniere with rear seat and fringed sunshade! All these bodies were similar in concept to those of the same name applied to early horse drawn vehicles, and generally speaking the cars were well made on conservative, well-tried lines - a characteristic of all FN cars throughout the period of production.

1902 saw the introduction of a further model, a 14hp four passenger tonneau - the first FN to offer shaft drive - and this was followed in 1905 by the large 30/40hp model, one of the most famous ever produced by the company, finding favour in luxurious, coachbuilt form with the Shah of Persia. This was the predecessor of another famous line - the Model 6900, both vehicles having four cylinder engines built under Rochet-Schneider

licence, the cylinders being cast in pairs. A disc type clutch was fitted, together with a four speed gearbox with conventional lever change, and again shaft drive was employed to a live rear axle with full differential. Semi-elliptic leaf spring suspension was augmented by an additional leaf spring mounted parallel to the axle beam, and steering was by worm and sector.

By 1909 car production was running at the rate of three or four a day (even in 1900 a hundred examples of the two cylinder voiturette had been made) and five cars a day were leaving the factory by 1914. The Model 2000 introduced some years after the 6900 incorporated some notable improvements, including a system of engine mounting by transverse bars and supports, magneto ignition with the distributor mounted forward of the camshaft and a fabric lined cone clutch. Otherwise the engine was the same as that offered in the 6900.

Improved suspension characterised the Model 2000A and 2100 which followed, although basically they were similar to the 2000, except that the

engine was mounted on a subframe.

Despite their conservatism, all FNs were well made of the best material and whilst not over luxurious, their coachwork reflected the refinement of beautifully engineered mechanics and chassis, all of which was offered at a reasonable price.

Development continued, however, and the company was not averse to motor sport as a means of advertising their products and improving the breed. Their first victory came in 1907 when Mathot achieved the then sensational speed of 70 mph on the Traject Ostend/Blankenberghe in a Model RS.

One of the attractions of the 1909 Paris Motor Show was the FN 1500 with reinforced chassis, improved carburettor and a floor mounted accelerator, and this was shortly followed by the 1600 which utilised a similar four cylinder engine but with increased bore, a re-designed gearbox and a sliding cardan shaft. The petrol tank was moved to the rear of the car, and suspension was again revised to improve the ride. This model in turn was superseded by the 2400, another

Economy class. The 1914 1250 first introduced in 1910 as a new line of small FNs. With large bore oversquare engine and the luxury of detachable wheels, the model was popular and in modified form was continued after the Great War. Few were made before the German invasion halted production.

Lengthened chassis, softer springs and a modified frontal treatment distinguish this post-First War 1250 A from its predecessor. Sporting lines, a cowled-in radiator, boat tail and dummy ship's ventilators on the scuttle were advanced features for the day although some of the hand controls still have to live outside.

four cylinder model with metal disc type clutch.

The types 2700 and 2700A heralded FN's move into the large car field, these being equipped with large capacity engines and foreign carburettors rather than those of their own manufacture. Strangely, at the same time, the company commenced the development of really small cars, the first of which appeared in 1910. Designated the 1250 and equipped with a leather lined cone clutch, a new small oversquare engine with a large bore and detachable wheels, this

The Rochet-Schneider ancestry of this 1908 RS model is unmistakable, although it wears FN's radiator badge. A large 'four' with pair cast cylinders, its large bodywork was well sprung by semi-elliptics with an auxiliary transverse rear spring.

This 1300 was first introduced in 1924, and for all its stolid appearance proved to be a best seller. This is a somewhat later version with balloon tyres, but the flush sided doors, devoid of door handles, give a particularly clean uncluttered line to the bodywork.

Fitted with sports fabric bodywork the 1.3 litre 1300 was a handsome car. Pushrod operated overhead valves, unit construction of engine and gearbox and front wheel brakes all helped to make this 1924 model really up to date. Note the dual windshields for driver and rear seat passengers and the American style step plates in place of conventional running boards.

Most luxurious of the vintage FNs was the 3800 here seen, exceptionally, in sedanca de ville form, complete with jump seats for servants or occasional passengers. A canvas 'roof' pulls forward to clip onto the windscreen to afford the chauffeur some protection. It was with this chassis that FN entered the commercial vehicle field.

boasted boat tailed bodywork of sporting appearance, and was enthusiastically received. Unfortunately, however, serious production was interrupted by the advent of World War One, although the model was destined to survive the war, and was revived following the Armistice. 1914 also witnessed an excursion to Brooklands where a single seater FN fitted with a 3400cc engine showed that for all its conservatism the marque could be rapid when it wished.

Despite the ravages of the war, and the fact that the factory at Herstal had been overrun by the Germans, the firm was soon in business once again after peace had been declared, producing, as before, orthodox models but utilising the new methods and techniques which had been learned during the war to improve their cars. Bodies became more streamlined, accessories which had been previously treated as extras were now fitted as standard, and suspensions were again improved still further. The electric starter came into its own, and with it electric lighting and increasing use of coil ignition.

In 1920 the 2700AT was introduced - a car which could compete with the best of the foreign models, which was fitted with an electric starter and lighting and an engine which, following aero engine practice, was made largely of aluminium. Fitted with a speedometer and with the luxury of automatic chassis lubrication, it helped to re-establish the company. Other models introduced at about the same time included the 1950, based on the pre-war 1600 and 2400, the 1200A, a modified version of the 1250, having a lengthened chassis and softened suspension and a higher mounted radiator. About a year later, a second version, the 1250T, put in an appearance, equipped with complete electrical system including starter, with chassis lengthened yet again and the radiator raised, but with identical

mechanical components. A four cylinder engine produced 10hp and the gearbox gave three forward speeds. In 1923, the final development was introduced as the 1250N, but the following year the whole line was discontinued and replaced by a completely redesigned light car - the 1300, which proved to be the company's great success of 1924. Fitted with a four cylinder 1500cc ohv engine with side mounted camshaft, having a bore and stroke of 65mm x 100mm, drive was taken through a disc type clutch and three speed box, and the model was offered in three variations - the 1300A, 1300B and 1300C, the mechanical components of all three being identical. Later

variations included the 1300D with a four speed box (also available with sports bodywork as the 1300 Sport) and the 1300E with wider track. Many of these were entered in international competitions with some success.

Shortly afterwards the 24hp 2150 was introduced with four speed gearbox and disc type clutch, and this also boasted automatic chassis lubrication, an oil pressure gauge was mounted on the instrument panel and a hypoid rear axle. Fitted with open four seater bodywork, this car had a respectable turn of speed and a sporting image. In 1925 the company fielded an entry in the Monte Carlo Rally and in the hands of Lieutenant

cylinders in line and shaft drive, and immediately before the Second World War they produced some very fine models, mainly for the Belgian Government, which eventually found their way into civilian hands in the post-war period, and many of which acquitted themselves well in competition.

During the twenties, however, FN cars enjoyed quite a vogue - particularly the 3800 and the 2200, the latter remaining available until 1924, and being the first of the smaller FNs with left hand drive and with both gear change and brake levers inside the body. Dynamo ignition was employed rather than a conventional magneto, echoing American practice, power being obtained from a 15hp 75mm x 125mm water-cooled four, and transmitted through a disc type clutch and four speed box to a hypoid rear axle. Rear wheel drum brakes only were fitted. Various bodies were available, including a van, and variations included the long chassis 2200E and the 2200F with four wheel brakes.

The late twenties saw a four cylinder 10hp model of 68mm x 100mm bore and stroke, with identical technical specification to the previous models, and from 1928 onwards extensive development work was carried out on its successor, the 11CV. Two prototypes of this model making the trip across the Black Continent in that year - the so-called *Raid au Caps* - in the first car were Lieutenants Fabry and Lamarche (of Monte Carlo and Tour de France fame), whilst the second car was driven by Monsieur Carton de Wiart and Monsieur Crouquet. In 1930, the 11CV was finally released to the public, announced as a Jubilee car to celebrate three decades of FN car manufacture. In final form it proved quite lively, four wheel braking ensuring that it stopped as well as it went, and among the full instrumentation were included the then innovative direction indicators. The engine was merely a development of the previous 10hp model and shared the same dimensions.

From this 11CV was derived the 1400 Sport (predecessor of the 1800 Sport) with similar specification and a small range of commercial vehicles with a 500kg payload were also based on this model.

Almost inevitably FN succumbed to eight cylinderitis in 1930, developing a

Lamarche reached third place in the general classification. They followed this in 1926 with a class win in the Tour de France, the driver again being Lieutenant Lamarche, and the car a 16CV 2200G, which continued in production until 1929.

Most luxurious of the vintage FNs was the 3800 available either as a drophead coupé or a torpedo (tourer) or in commercial form as a van or a lorry. The latter types were given a specially strengthened chassis, stronger axles, balloon tyres and stiffer suspension, and with this model FN entered the commercial vehicle field in which, these days, they are remembered.

For the remainder of the twenties and the early thirties, however, Fabrique Nationale concentrated upon cars for the middle and lower middle class, becoming mechanically quite advanced in specification - perhaps a little too advanced - during the early thirties, this perhaps being the reason for their failure during the economic Depression of the thirties.

Although car production ceased in 1935, however, the company had diversified at an early date, introducing motorcycles in 1905, and a variety of other products throughout the years, and the stringencies of the Depression period did not, therefore, bankrupt the company. Their motorcycles particularly are remembered for their excellent quality, four vertical

The 11CV introduced to the public in 1930 to mark the thirtieth year of FN car production. Designated the Jubilee car, two prototypes of this model had made trips across the 'Black Continent' in 1928. The bonnet louvres are reminiscent of Standard during the same period but the bodywork is pure Detroit.

Attractive lines again. The 1800 Sport for 1930, wearing a very American stoneguard for the radiator and step plates reminiscent of the 1924 1300 Sport. Other Americanisms are a Boyce style Motormeter on the radiator cap and tubular front bumper.

Eight cylinderitis. Lord Montagu's theory that the straight eight engine coupled with the Depression was the shortest route to Carey Street may not have been strictly true of FN since their resources were not only dependent upon cars. It was almost the end of the road for the car division, however.

Straight Eight side valve with a bore and stroke of 72mm x 100mm (3250cc) and a nett rating of 17hp. This car gained some prizes in contests and races, although production models were fitted with a rather heavy body, and these sporting performances complemented Weerens and Nathot's performance in a non-stop trip over the 3300 kms on the Rallye Liege/Madrid/Liege.

In 1931 an improved 11CV - the 1625 - was introduced with larger capacity engine with rubber mountings. Steering was by worm and sector and the frame was given greater stiffness. In the same year, three FNs were entered for the Coupe des Alpes, crewed by Collignon and Malbrant, Charlier and Bove, and George and Nelissen respectively, each driving an excellent race and taking first, second and third in their class with the 1625. In the same year, and with the same model, Collignon and Bove took first place in the Budapest Rally. A year later and as a publicity stunt drivers Collignon, Malbrant, George and Detaille piloted a Straight Eight non-stop from Brussels to Gibraltar, covering the distance in eight hours less than the fastest express train had previously recorded.

The company entered the 24 Heures de Francorchamps on four separate occasions, and each time were successful. In 1925 and 1926 a 1300 took a 'first', whilst in 1932 the honours fell to a Straight Eight, followed in 1933 with a win in a Baudouin model.

From the early thirties, FN appeared to have succumbed to the same disease which afflicted Singer, offering no less than 16 different models, covering all sectors of the market, and in 1932 offered their first eight cylinder commercial chassis with a payload of 1½ tons, and utilising the same engine as the car. This chassis was also offered to bus operators and in 1933 FN began to specialise in heavy commercial vehicles and the manufacture of trolleybuses for the city of Liege, although the electrical parts were manufactured by Belgium's largest producer of electrical equip-

ment, CEB. Some of these buses are apparently still in service in the same municipality.

The Baudouin which was so successful in the 24 Heures de Francorchamps made its appearance in 1933 as a replacement for the 1625, offering a two litre, four cylinder engine with 79.9mm x 100mm bore and stroke, and a top speed of 100 kph. Suspension, which was very soft, took the form of long leaf springs fitted with shock absorbers, but this was to be almost the last car which FN produced.

Their swansong was to be the Prince Albert, with virtually identical specification to the Baudouin but with more spacious five seater bodywork, and a slightly larger engine of 85mm x 100mm (2260cc). Modern lines characterised this car, the last of which left the production line in 1935.

During the Second World War the works were nearly totally destroyed, and much of the equipment was taken over by the Germans, but with the liberation came work repairing Allied military equipment, and in 1946 production of commercial vehicles recommenced. These were continued up until about five years ago, when the decision was taken to discontinue civilian types, and to concentrate on military models, which the company had been producing since 1955. Currently, the company's vehicle production is concentrated upon the Type AS, a three wheeled airborne carrier, lightweight and easy to parachute and capable of transporting four soldiers or a 300kg load, and it is arousing interest in many countries.

For all the fact that FN vehicles were always produced in reasonably high numbers, two wars have taken their toll and few have survived. Veteran car clubs in Belgium, Holland and Great Britain boast a few among their members, and the National Museum van de Automobiel at Driebergen fortunately preserves a 1900 Victoria tonneau - one of the first production models - and a Prince Albert is believed to have survived in the United States.

THE REBIRTH OF AN AC

This is not just another average restoration story, or even the log of an historic car, but an account of the somewhat unusual career of a 1928 six cylinder AC Acedes. DAVID HALES, better known for his writings on ABC, Bean, Vulcan and other member companies of the British Motor Trading Corporation, has been delving into the fascinating history of the car he is rebuilding. It will serve to whet the appetites of enthusiasts until John McLellan's history of the marque appears in the *KALEIDOSCOPE* series in the Autumn.

HAVING sold my vintage 1925 ABC Supersports car, I was looking for a suitable replacement which might prove a little more practical, but without causing an undue strain on the bank balance. I kept an eye on the usual monthly magazines for such likely candidates as 12/50 Alvis, two litre Lagonda, etc, but nothing I could afford, or liked, seemed to be around

at the time, so I started looking a little wider. I had noticed an advert in *Exchange & Mart* for a 1930s two litre AC, and although this particular specimen required far too much work for me to entertain, it did make me think seriously about the suitability of this marque from the 1930s.

This, however, was an avenue largely unexplored, and I didn't know

of anyone locally from whom I could seek advice, although there had been a local vintage AC owner for some years. I therefore paid him a casual visit in Kingston-Upon-Thames to ask if he had ever had any experience of 1930s ACs and although I didn't come away much wiser about the subject of my enquiry, he did say that the only AC he had ever owned was a 1927 six

PH 8013 as it started life, and in unmodified form, when owned by Watford orchid grower, Mrs Sander. Finished in nutria and champagne it was supplied in March 1928 as a standard two seater with dickey. Note the fixed starting handle. The side mounted spare wheel and 'stepped down' running board echoes the design of the Cubitt model K in which AC's guiding light, S F Edge, also had a hand.

PK 6322 with Thames Ditton toolroom manager A J Mollart at the wheel displaying trophies picked up during the 1928 season. This was the specially prepared Montlhéry which the Hon Victor Bruces used for their successful record-breaking attempts at the French track in 1927 and which Mollart purchased after it had returned to the works.

cylinder two litre Montlhéry, which he had had for the past 26 years, and would consider selling should I be interested.

I hadn't enthused over the back axle gearbox arrangements of the vintage ACs, so instead of making a hasty decision I asked the Vintage Registrar of the ACOC about the 'type', including another car being advertised by a London dealer. I was advised against the latter, and since nothing else had turned up meanwhile, I decided to go and have a look at the Montlhéry, which was kept in Suffolk. The car was basically sound, although it had been on blocks in the garage for twelve years, and there had been a number of obvious changes to the specification

over the years. There was nothing that couldn't be put right, however, (preferably whilst running the car on the road) so a figure was agreed and I became the new owner of PH 8013.

Whilst collecting the AC by trailer, the previous owner, Lt Col Michael Dracopoli, mentioned that he thought that the car was the one used by the Hon Victor Bruces for their marathon at the Montlhéry track. Since, however, so many cars are advertised today as being 'genuine' racing cars, or having a 'genuine' history, but are merely replicas or of a similar type to a car that did have a history, I was sceptical to say the least.

The first job on my list, apart from a general tidy-up of the car, was to gather what information I could about its original specification, both from manufacturers' catalogues and previous owners. Catalogues and press reports of the period were fairly straightforward, and most of the information concerning what the car should look like was soon solved. Contacting previous owners took a little longer, but has now been accomplished with the following interesting results, which are recounted in chronological order:-

As a standard two seater and dickey, finished in nutria and champagne, it was supplied in March 1928 to a Mrs Sander, an orchid

grower from near Watford, Hertfordshire, although, as frequently occurs, the vehicle was registered in its county of origin, in this case Surrey - PH 8013. Her son, who now lives in the Isle of Wight, informed me that this was the fourth or fifth AC his parents had owned, and although it was registered under his mother's name, in fact it belonged to his father. Even so, his mother regularly used the car, even participating in one or two modest rallies.

After about two years the car was returned to the factory at Thames Ditton, presumably in an exchange deal, and another AC followed it in 1930. A potential customer at the works early in 1930 was R J P Morley, who was persuaded to take the two seater at an advantageous price, since the company were in Receivership by this time and very anxious to sell everything they could!

Ray Morley was then living with his parents at Dunsmoor House, Wendover, and his father, although not terribly enthusiastic about motor cars for their own sake, had owned a number of ACs, and being a keen sportsman himself was most emphatic that his son should compete in some form of sport. Therefore, after familiarising himself with the intricacies of a four cylinder AC of 1920 which his father had bought for him in

1924, the six cylinder 16/40 represented a step in the right direction. Even so, it would be better still if the performance were improved and the coachwork lightened.

But what of the Montlhéry sports model used by the Hon Victor Bruce, his wife and J A Joyce to capture the series of records at the French track in December 1927? The Bruces were well known for their various AC activities, but had always used more touring mounts. Not surprisingly, when a Montlhéry version was seen in a London showroom, it was decided that it would be the type of vehicle in which to attempt further records, and as a result it was returned to Thames Ditton, where it was carefully stripped and prepared for its ordeal.

The eventual outcome is already well known, though following its successful foray it returned to the works once more, after which the Bruces never saw the car again. At that time (December 1927) A J Mollart was toolroom manager at Thames Ditton, and it was he who bought the car and registered it on the road in 1928 as PK 6322. In this form it looked exactly like a standard catalogued Montlhéry car, but with the optional wire wheels (instead of discs), and three carburettors.

By the end of 1928 the car, with A J Mollart driving, had accumulated an impressive array of cups, tankards, silver spoons and medals, and during the course of 1929 the Montlhéry body was removed, complete with V windscreen, and replaced with a specially designed fabric four seater touring body with fold-flat screen and two aero screens for the purpose of competing in the Brooklands Double Twelve Race. This left a spare body which was duly advertised for sale, at which time Ray Morley entered the scene again, eager to modify his own chassis.

By this time A J Mollart had left ACs, as had many another old hand, and started his own engineering works at Albany Reach, Thames Ditton, and it was from these works that the Montlhéry body was collected in 1929, to fit onto the chassis of PH 8013. Back at Wendover, the coachwork was swapped over, though the touring mudguards and lamps were retained. A new set of wire wheels were acquired from the works to replace the discs, and after a few months initial usage

Brighton Speed Hill Climb - 1930. PH 8013, fitted with the Montlhéry body, awaits the starter's flag, followed by another AC. Coincidentally, Mollart was also exercising the fabric four seater at the Brighton event and with the latter's sportier ratios and triple carbs he romped away with a first and three seconds.

with the original carburettor, triple carbs were fitted at the works by Mr Pugh during 1931.

The Lucas headlamps were fitted with wire stoneguards bought from Vic Derrington, and at a later date were augmented by two Raydyot spot lamps mounted either side of the screen with mirrors on the back. The side lamps were eventually changed to 1930s style torpedo type, and a fog lamp was attached to the front number plate.

Since it was intended to use the car for trials rather than speed work, the original touring ratios of the gearbox and back axle were retained, as was most of the original dashboard including Smith's 8-day clock, Lucas ammeter, switch box and oil gauge. Since some fairly high revs were intended to be used in trials, and the car suffered from a three speed box, a rev counter was thought rather inappropriate in case it scared the life

out of the driver! At a later date a Tapley gradient meter and a small brake meter were fitted. The original disappearing hood was retained - not that it mattered a great deal since it was never used by its new owner - waterproof clothing being deemed adequate, though a tonneau cover was made for the car. Audible warning was provided by the original Klaxon, to which was added a three note bulb horn, and an electric bell on the running board - much frowned on by the police!

From the start the upper parts of the ex-Bruce car had been finished in maroon (Mercedes red?) with matching mudguards and polished aluminium lower parts. In its new guise it retained the same body finish, but of course now had the standard touring mudguards repainted black, the old touring body being left at a blacksmith's shop in Wendover. The remaining months of 1930 were spent in getting used to the new outfit, but amongst events entered was the Brighton Rally in which A J Mollart was also exercising the fabric four seater. The latter romped away, with sportier ratios, and at that time the advantage of triple carbs, thus gaining a 1st and three 2nd awards.

During 1931 some 14 events were

entered, including such familiar sorties as the London-Edinburgh, Land's End-John O'Groats, London-Gloucester, London-Exeter, and the Ulster Club's Dover-Belfast, as well as numerous lesser affairs, from which 13 awards were gained. Much the same format applied for the next few years with considerable success up to 1934, during which year the highlight must have been the outright win in the RAC Rally, all of which was well recorded by motoring photographer W J Brunell. It was during the latter part of its competition career that it acquired the cut-out by the driver's right elbow to allow easier manoeuvrability round tight corners, though it hardly improved its appearance.

For the latter part of 1934 and the next few years, things were a bit quieter for PH 8013, and on 22nd April 1938 it was once again sold back to the works at Thames Ditton for £25, which, less selling commission to the next owner, left Ray Morley with the princely sum of £22-10-0d, which was put towards an ex-works 16/80 Competition two seater, registered EPK 667 (which also survives today in the United States).

At Thames Ditton the AC works were, of course, now under new management, W A E Hurlock being

PK 6322 as fitted with the Double Twelve four seater body. This specially designed fabric touring style with fold-flat screen and two aero screens was Mollart's replacement for the original Montlhéry body, and in this form the car competed in the Double Twelve race at Brooklands.

PH 8013 as acquired by Michael Dracopoli. The car had been considerably modified by previous owner Ian Girling, a friend of Derek Hurlock, the then AC Managing Director's son. Cycle type wings were substituted and the spare wheel relegated to the boot. Note the relocated outside handbrake - the gear lever was centralised - and the fold-flat windscreen and aero screens.

Managing Director, and his son Derek serving his apprenticeship there. One of Derek's friends back at the Suffolk family home near Ipswich was Ian Girling, and whilst PH 8013 remained at the works unsold, Derek used the car back and forth to Suffolk where Ian became a frequent passenger. He must have been suitably impressed since he purchased the car later in 1938.

Of course it was now ten years old and had been fairly well used, and was beginning to look a little tired. There was also, as it turned out, very little time in which to carry on using it before Mr Hitler put his oar in, and stopped many an enthusiast's pastime.

Ian Girling joined the RAF and the AC became considerably less used. Age, however, was catching up on her; the running boards were rotting, causing insufficient support for the mudguards and these, in turn, became loose. The central cast aluminium V screen support also broke, with the result that the screen was removed and replaced by a fold-flat screen and twin aero screens, both mounted on a modified scuttle line. The old touring mudguards were also removed together with the running boards, and aluminium cycle wings were fitted. The spare wheel having thus lost its mounting, was relegated to the dickey seat. The dashboard was also later modified, as a result of the uplifting of the timber behind the steering column support, which deposited the wheel in the driver's lap!

A new dashboard was made up in which some of the original instruments were used, but to which were added a number of switches and dials courtesy of HM Forces. In the course of time, brakes and handling were improved by the fitting of a Riley front axle with larger diameter brakes, and a Riley steering wheel. The handbrake was moved from inside the body on the right hand side to a position outside the body, and the gear lever re-installed centrally, also being made removable as a thief-proof parking aid! All this, of course, took time; the war had come to an end, and there was a pretty young girl. Something

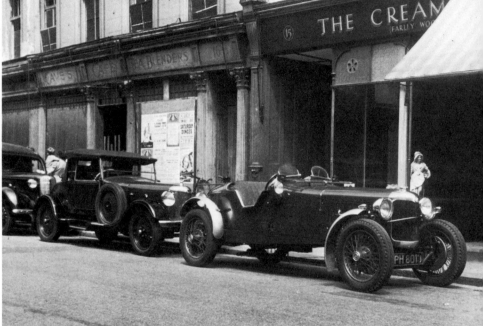

PH 8013 subsequently acquired triple carbs also during later ownerships and the photograph of the engine compartment shown here illustrates the uncluttered and businesslike power unit. The cycle type wings can also be seen.

During the time the car was in Ian Girling's hands, PH 8013 suffered the splitting of timber behind the steering wheel support [which deposited the driving wheel in his lap!] and this led to the re-design of the whole dashboard as illustrated here. Although some of the original instruments were incorporated, a number of additional switches and dials were added by courtesy of HM Forces!

As purchased by David Hales, PH 8013 bears an uncanny resemblance to the Bishop Specials built on modified Ford T chassis by Bishops Garages in the mid-twenties - even down to the bullnosed radiator and cycle type wings. So far, the engine has been rebuilt, new mudguards to original Montlhéry specification are being made, and the fold-flat screen will be replaced with a suitable vee screen.

had to go, so the AC was sold again in 1951 to finance a home, the new owner being Lt Col Michael Dracopoli, whose family home was also in the Ipswich area.

At the time Michael Dracopoli was serving with The Buffs and stationed in East Anglia, but was soon moved to East Kent where the AC provided daily transport. He explained to members of the AC Owners Club that the previous owner, although of a mechanical bent, was no purist, and over the course of the next few years the correct AC front axle was re-instated, some of the lamps removed (including the two Raydyot spots), the Fram oil cooler was dispensed with and the car generally tidied up, including reupholstery. Most of this work was undertaken whilst he journeyed the world with his military duties, which prevented much use of the AC, so since 1955 the car has had little use. In 1965, a new set of axle stands were bought, and the car placed on these in the family home near Ipswich until my visit in 1977.

It was my intention to use the car on the road almost straightaway, after having a new petrol tank made to overcome a 'rusty petrol' problem. One or two other faults, however, have delayed taking to the road quite so soon, and the radiator needs attention, the engine has been rebuilt and new mudguarding and running boards are underway. A new V screen also requires making - unless any reader can supply one from another car? Whilst undertaking this work I am using the opportunity to return the car to something like the original Montlhéry specification, eventually, if cash permits, making up the correct gear ratios for a better top speed performance, but that's a while away yet. I would like to thank all the previous owners of PH 8013 for their assistance with information and photographs, and to the Hon Mrs Victor Bruce and K Mollart (who now runs Mollart Engineering on the Kingston By-Pass, which his father set up in 1935) for the early history of PK 6322. It would be interesting to find out what happened to the latter car, which as far as I can make out has not been seen since before World War II. Does any reader have any further information on this car?

IT'S
NEW
it's the
Scootacar
DE LUXE

THE BUBBLE
THAT BURST

**It is a popular myth that the Suez crisis with its subsequent petrol rationing in 1956
spawned the 'bubble car' boom. Certainly it added impetus to it, but in fact
the most successful contenders for the microcar market were, with few exceptions,
already well entrenched by the time that Gamul Nasser decided to flex
his nationalist muscles and bring down upon his head the wrath of France,
aided by Israeli and British 'police action'. THE EDITOR has been looking at
the post-war rise and fall in the popularity of the ultra-economy car.**

THE first fact which emerges from a
broad study of the first fifteen years
following the Second World War is
that history most decidedly repeats
itself. Very probably every era
produces its crop of rather unorthodox
designs, but it is apparently only

under extreme conditions that they
surface briefly, proliferate, then fade
away with the return to normality.
Thus we find parallels in, for example,
the various permutations of Marcel
Violet's wayward inventiveness during
the first cyclecar era and the extra-

ordinary confections from the drawing
board of post-war protagonist Laurie
Bond. Both flew in the face of
accepted design principles, both had a
hand in the design of several makes,
and both enjoyed limited success and
never seemed to run out of willing and

One of the few wholly British bubblecars, the Scootacar [not to be confused with the pre-war Rytecraft Scootacar] hailed from Leeds and was made between 1957 and 1964. Offered initially with a 197cc Villiers engine, it later graduated to 346cc and in this form was said to accommodate two adults and a child. It was, however, incredibly cramped and suffered - unlike its German counterparts - from a high centre of gravity. £5 Road Tax a year and running costs claimed of 1¼d [pre-decimal] per mile were advantages, however.

optimistic sponsors.

Violet himself was still in the lists as late as 1946 with the 4CV Bernadette, a three seater roadster with a transverse front mounted 798cc water-cooled four which pre-dated Issognis by thirteen years, but this was rarely seen outside the Paris and Geneva salons and on the Continent the most persistent purveyor of unorthodoxy was Egon Brutsch. His curious little egg shaped cars hailed from Germany, although they appeared from time to time elsewhere endowed with different names and nationalities.

All were based on the Zwerg (dwarf), a monocoque three wheeler with tubular framing, rubber suspension, mechanical brakes, a choice of motorcycle type engines and scooter sized wheels. The 200cc variant was capable of 65 mph for those with the courage to try it.

Minimal motoring in the extreme was, however, provided by Brutsch's Mopetta, launched on an unsuspecting public in 1957. Powered by a 50cc Ilo engine mounted alongside the driver (no room for passengers), the car cost £200 and boasted three gears, no differential, and chain drive to one rear wheel. Bodywork was of plastic and overall length only 69 inches. The front of the car was fitted with a handle which enabled it to be wheeled along on the twin rear wheels like a shopping trolley - very handy for manoeuvring it into odd little parking spaces too small for the average motorcycle.

A four wheeler, the Pfeil, had appeared a year earlier and during two years of production it was sponsored by both the Bavarian based Spatz concern, and latterly by the German Victoria motorcycle firm whose name it adopted. With tubular backbone and the well-tried 200cc Sachs engine mounted at the rear (later the Victoria 248cc) about 1500 Spatz were built, and in two seater form were quite attractive.

It could be said, of course, that Germany was the spiritual home of the unorthodox small car. Cyclecars of all shapes and sizes were made there during the twenties - far longer, in fact, than elsewhere and doubtless

The British Anzani powered Astra turned up in many guises. As the Jarc it utilised a 250cc Excelsior Talisman twin two stroke prior to the British Anzani takeover, and later appeared as the Gill Getabout two seater with the engine mounted at the rear.

COMMERCIAL CAR

Combines

- **UTILITY**
- **PERFORMANCE**
- **APPEARANCE**
- **ECONOMY**

. . . at the RIGHT PRICE

Countless Travellers, Tradesmen and Service Engineers have welcomed this comfortable, easy-to-drive all-purpose vehicle. Powered by British Anzani 322 c.c. Twin two-stroke unit for economical running, with everything easily accessible for maintenance, and with exceptional goods space, it is the perfect answer to most light transport problems.

£347:16s.
(Incl. Commercial P.T.)

Back raised for easy loading

60 MILES Per Gallon **58** MILES Per Hour

 Write to the Manufacturers for illustrated brochure.

BRITISH ANZANI ENGINEERING CO. LTD., HAMPTON HILL, MIDDX. (MOL 2690)

Clockwork Orange - the Peel Trident.

helped by Germany's chaotic finances following the collapse of the mark in 1922. The theme was continued throughout the thirties, however, with Josef Ganz occupying a similar rôle to that enjoyed by Brutsch after the war. At least two firms, and probably more, who fielded economy models from 1948 onwards owed something to Ganz. Holbein's Champion in original prototype form was more or less a carbon copy of Ganz' ideas - two seater body, backbone frame with swing axle suspension and small motorcycle type engine - whilst Wilhelm Gutbrod's firm had made Ganz' Standard Superior until 1939 although admittedly his 1949 Gutbrod Superior owed little to its predecessor, and the 593cc two stroke twin which drove the front wheels was his own.

Strangely, Italy did not take the minicar to its heart after the war, and one suspects that despite the economies which the ravages of war dictated, the average Italian driver preferred the relative sophistication of Fiat's Topolino - an established model pre-war as well - to anything which the two stroke and fibreglass brigade were advocating at the time. Beyond the three wheeler Piaggio truck - based on their Scooter (which was successfully licence produced as the Vespa by Douglas in Great Britain) - Italy's contribution rested mainly upon Iso's Isetta.

Although it was to prove perhaps the most successful of the 'bubble' type cars, and could even be said to have started the fashion, the Isetta enjoyed only three seasons in its native Milan, no Isos being built between 1955 and 1962 and those appearing latterly being Euro-American GT saloons bearing no relation to the Isetta. The Isetta design was, however, taken up enthusiastically by VELAM in France and BMW in Germany. BMW were, of course, no strangers to licence produced small cars, their 1930's Dixi being an Eisenach-built Austin Seven, and they proved the most successful. Eschewing Iso's original 236cc air-cooled two stroke twin (with Trojan-like common combustion chamber), they favoured their own single cylinder four stroke, and continued to make the car from 1954 until 1963. Isetta of Great Britain in turn took out a licence from BMW and from 1957 until 1964 built two and four

(with close coupled rear wheels) wheelers in the old London Brighton & South Coast Railway engine sheds at Brighton (Stroudley, doubtless, turned in his grave) and altogether more than 36,000 were built in various countries.

Naturally, there were imitators, and the most flagrant of these must have been J O Hoffman, a Vespa agent from Lintorf. Mr Hoffman fondly imagined that if he simply copied an Isetta and replaced the latter's front opening single door with a side opening single door, neither Milan nor Munich would have anything to grouse about. His dream lasted just three months in 1954, during which time he managed to deliver 113 of his Auto-Kabines before patent infringement litigation put him out of business.

Piaggio were not the only aircraft manufacturers to see salvation in the economy market, however, and just as Graham-White, ABC, Sopwith and Kingsbury had done in 1919 with their scooters and cyclecars, so Ernst Heinkel, Willi Messerschmidt and the son of Claude Dornier turned to the Bubble car.

The Heinkel Cabin Cruiser most nearly followed the configuration of the Isetta, except that both ends swung up, but unlike the Isetta (the steering wheel of which was attached to the front opening door with complicated jointing), the steering column was attached to the door pillar. Commencing as a three wheeler, it acquired a fourth in 1957, featured hydraulically operated brakes on the front wheels only and fielded an overhead valve single cylinder engine of own manufacture which at 174cc was somewhat smaller than the Isetta. Here again, as with the Iso, the home demand proved small and in three

Not an ME109, but a Tg500 Messerschmidt in 1960. This four wheeled version, the Tiger, was built from 1958 until 1960 with 500cc Sachs twin cylinder engine, could show a clean pair of heels to most of its contemporaries and earned praise from John Bolster. FMR stood for *F*ahrzeug und *M*aschinenbau GmBH, *R*egensburg. The Messerschmidt was virtually the only bubble car to employ a side opening 'lid'. Owners new to the car and unfamiliar with it were not unknown to trap themselves inside!

years only a little over 6000 units found buyers in Germany. Licence production once again came to the rescue, and whilst the Dundalk Engineering version sold in the Irish Republic made little impression, that built by Trojan in Great Britain (a firm who were certainly no strangers to unorthodoxy - one feels that Leslie Hounsfield would have approved) under the Trojan name survived until 1965 and was even sold as a light van!

It was in 1953 that Messerschmidt

commenced manufacture of their version of the marginal motor, and as befits the manufacturer of the Bf110 its tandem seating, joystick control and general aircraft cockpit appearance was allied to performance and handling which drew praise from the contemporary sporting press. Although only 99 inches long and 48 inches wide, it was quite the fastest of the Bubbles, and capable of over 60 mph. Despite its aircraft background, however, its general design was not derived from anything Willi built during the war, but from a cheap type of invalid carriage devised by Fritz Rosenheim in 1948 for the use of disabled ex-servicemen. In this there is a parallel with the 1919 Landini cyclecar designed by a flying instructor for disabled flyers, and also featuring tandem seating, rudder bar control and foot steering!

Initially a three wheeler, the

Messerschmidt later acquired, like its fellows, a fourth wheel and transmitted the drive from its 174cc Sachs two stroke single cylinder rear-mounted engine via a chain to the rear wheel. Later versions utilised a 191cc engine, featured a rear dual seat (for children, presumably) and the marque actually sold the highest number of cars the year before Suez, with 11,909 delivered in 1955. Total production, which continued until 1962, ran to well over 30,000 units, which compares favourably with the Isetta.

Dornier's Delta was a peculiar little vehicle, licence production for which was taken up by motorcycle producers Zundapp of Nuremberg. They renamed it the Janus, after the Roman God who faced two ways, and appositely, too. More angular than either the Isetta or the Heinkel, it featured front and rear opening doors, the rear set of seats facing backwards.

Iso's Isetta. Vested interests at Fiat and in the motorcycle and scooter industry prevented much more than a lukewarm reception for Iso's popular mini-car. It was left to BMW to make a real success of it, and the British version built at Brighton derived from the Bavarian derivative. This 1955 Italian model is seen taking part in the Mille Miglia.

The 248cc two stroke engine was mounted amidships between the two sets of seats, an arrangement which permitted the accommodation of four people in a space which would only normally carry two.

Fitted with Zundapp's own engine and boasting unitary construction of engine and gearbox, four speeds and independent rear suspension, it was even imported into Britain. Such a formula, however, proved even too much for the long suffering marginal motorist and, introduced in 1956, the Janus lasted only until 1957. At £556 it was some £70 more expensive than the current Ford Anglia and very little cheaper than a Prefect and, after all, *dos à dos* went out before the turn of the century.

There were, of course, other makes Laurie Bond has already been mentioned. His Bond Minicar appeared in 1948 - an ugly, underpowered two seater plus kids, totally

reminiscent of the Stafford Cripps austerity era in which it was born, but which was nevertheless destined to a life of seventeen years. Its original 122cc two stroke Villiers engine was mounted above the single front wheel, to which it drove through a three speed gearbox without reverse. The engine turned with the wheel, enabling the little machine to turn in its own length rather like a fairground dodg'em car, and its stressed aluminium skin and unitary construction made it so light that it replaced the Austin Seven as the subject of practical jokes by exuberant students. I recall the evening on which a perplexed owner, having reported his car stolen, perceived it dangling by a single rope from the top of the flag pole outside the Downs Hotel, Keymer in Sussex. It was lowered as simply as it had been hoisted, and was none the worse for its adventure.

In more sporting vein, Laurie's Berkeley was designed for Charles Panter's Biggleswade based caravan manufacturing company, and appeared in 1956. Built up from bolted-up fibreglass and powered by an air-cooled 322cc British Anzani two stroke (later replaced by the 328cc Excelsior), top speed was 65 mph and

What the Purley Way was doing between 1962 and 1965. The Trojan was nothing more than a revived Heinkel, production having ceased in Germany in 1958. Optimistically offered as a light van, too, the design was also adopted by Dundalk Engineering in the Irish Republic in 1958, but little was heard of this venture.

the car would cruise at 60. Despite crudities of construction, the general lines were attractive, giving the car the looks of a scaled down full sized sports car, and the marque enjoyed four seasons before succumbing in 1960. A three wheeler was also produced during the same period.

Another Bond design to use the British Anzani engine was the Unicar, built at Boreham by S E Opperman Ltd and, like the Berkeley, utilising a fibreglass body. Drive was by chain via an Albion gearbox to a solid rear axle, but suspension was quite sophisticated with Girling struts at the front and a swing-axle device at the rear. Offered in kit form, with hire purchase from Bowmaker Ltd included in the package, later versions - the Stirling - offered the Steyr-Puch 500 engine. In kit form, however, the car cost £265 in 1958 in which year a Ford Popular cost only £443 and by 1959 Opperman (facing the BMC Mini, too) gave up the unequal struggle.

One could go on. There was the Gordon, financed by the profits from Vernon's football pools, and designed by Erling Poppe, who designed the S7 and S8 shaft driven motorcycles for Sunbeam and who ought to have known better. Looking rather like an angular version of the Bond, the Gordon managed to incorporate all its vices and none of its virtues. The 197cc Villiers it used in common with the Bond was located awkwardly to the offside of the frame amidships, requiring a bulge in the panelling to accommodate the chain drive. Described as a four seater, but barely capable, with its weight of 716 lbs, of propelling two adults at anything like a reasonable pace, it was fairly cheap at £270 and received a boost from Suez, which kept it going until 1958.

Of the remainder, most were pretty horrible and best forgotten from an engineering standpoint if nothing else. The ugly little Rodley - an angular little coupé powered by 750cc vee twin JAP - hailed from Leeds and acquired an unenviable reputation for setting itself on fire, the AC Petite gave the old established Thames Ditton firm the doubtful distinction of manufacturing both the fastest and the slowest production cars in Britain - its vee belt primary drive was cyclecarism *par excellence* and its noisy 346cc Villiers engine ran hot. AC were not the only sports car manufacturers to try the mini market, however, Allard's Clipper being described by *Motor Sport* as a 'return to the cyclecar'. An all-plastic egg, the Clipper copied AC's belt primary drive, accommodated two adults in its coupé body by

Hordern-Richmond and, optimistically, two children in a dickey seat. At £267 it sold about 30 units before Allard saw sense.

The Powerdrive was the result of the Clipper's designer, David Gottlieb, moving on to Wood Green after Allard had shown him the door, and once again the 322cc Anzani was employed. The result was a miniature convertible of somewhat transatlantic lines with a lion's head grille motif which looked like someone's door knocker. The

Tourette was sponsored by a Surrey based firm of Messerschmidt dealers, and incorporated a fair number of their parts in its construction and was basically another variation of the Brutsch theme.

The Scootacar lasted quite respectably - from 1957 until 1964, in fact - which is surprising when one considers the specification. Built in Leeds like the Rodley, it was basically an enclosed scooter, albeit with three wheels, and was therefore much

Just like the cyclecar before it, the bubble car became the butt of many jokes and this seaside postcard is just one of many which kept holiday-makers chuckling and which, like the Model T jokes which old Henry is said to have encouraged, probably did the industry no harm. Best remembered is, perhaps, Brockbank's immortal [and, as usual, enraged] Major Upsett booting, like a football, an offending example confronting him on a zebra crossing.

Cousin to the motor scooter, the French two stroke rear engined Vespa.

"Turn over to the other shide. I'm fed up with these sloppy love programmes.'

built Frisky deserved a better fate. I have fond memories of a lift back to my RAF camp in the prototype on the eve of the Geneva Show at which it was announced in 1957. Its gull-wing doors were reminiscent of the Mercedes 300 SL (the similarity stopped there!) but it accommodated me, the driver, an RAF chum and our two kitbags quite comfortably, and the 249cc Villiers two stroke propelled us along quite briskly. Five company reorganisations later, the final bankruptcy came in 1964.

Prize for the most unlikely? That clockwork orange from the Isle of Man, named, appositely, the Peel. Rather like a mobile Dalek, the P50 made its belated debut at the 1962 Earl's Court Motorcycle Show, accommodated a single person and was powered by a 50cc DKW engine. The later Trident boasted side by side seats, a 4.2 bhp fan-cooled two stroke engine and three forward speeds, the whole bubble body hinging forward at the front to enable entry and exit from the vehicle. In its final form, it resembled a large motorcycle crash helmet. But about 100 found homes.

Undoubtedly, the BMC Mini, announced in 1959, sounded the death knell of the bubblecar and its contemporary economy cars as surely as its predecessor, the Austin Seven, effectively stifled the cyclecar after 1922 but the micro-car is remarkably resilient and bounced back in various forms in the thirties, and in electric guise in Occupied France in the forties.

Mark you, we haven't seen the last of either bubbles or eggs. With the final energy crisis only just around the corner, so we are told, it is inevitable that eventually we shall return - perhaps irrevocably - to the mini-car. After all, it has been proved time and again in the past that when we have to, we can and do take to the mini-car in a big way. With a little extra effort we could even enjoy it.

I should like to take this opportunity of thanking Peter Roberts; Michael Sedgwick; Tony Marshall and M E Thomas, who between them probably have the most complete collection of micro-cars in Britain; Hanns Peter Rosellen; and Ian Andrews of the Messerschmidt Owners' Club for information and photographs, without which this article would not have been possible.

higher than, say, the Messerschmidt and the rear seat was very cramped. Allied to a narrow track, the Scooter-car's high centre of gravity cannot have helped its stability.

Of the rest, the Astra, Jarc and Gill Getabout were all variations of the basic British Anzani theme, the Coronet from Denham, Bucks, another Anzani confection similar to the Powerdrive and the Nobel 200 just one phase in the life of the German-originated Fuldamobil which, during

a chequered career, was built by a subsidiary of the Bristol Aeroplane Company, Harland & Woolf, the Northern Ireland shipbuilders, and the ill fated Lea-Francis concern. It was also built in Chile as the Bambi, India as the Hans Vahaar and in Greece as the Attica, although quite why this 200cc Ilo engined Bubble should have found so many sponsors until as late as 1970 is something of a mystery.

Henry Meadows' Wolverhampton

BOB DICKER & THE AUTOTRIX

Generally speaking, the myriad ephemeral cyclecars which burst on the scene between 1910 and 1925 remain shadowy names in the Buyer's Guide and little more. Recently, however, we were fortunate to meet a spritely octogenarian who was not only able to throw a little light on one of them, but also managed to recapture for us some of the carefree atmosphere which was Brooklands before the Great War. His recent death after a short illness severs one more link with those early days.

BOB DICKER was born in 1892, a fact which was belied by his lively memory and his party trick of kicking his leg to shoulder height! At the age of 15 he was apprenticed to Shanks racing department at Brooklands and by 1908 was competing there himself. He won his second race at 42.8 mph riding a Chater-Lea.

His apprenticeship was scheduled to last seven years, as was usual in those days, but because of the free and easy atmosphere which prevailed, it was quite normal for him to be 'loaned' to other firms. Thus at various times he found himself working for the

Weybridge Gauge and Tool Company (the Competition Department of Zenith Motors Ltd - makers of Zenith motorcycles) and F E Barker, motor engineer - initially for 4/- per week!

Under a similar arrangement he was also seconded for a period to a shoe-string enterprise rejoicing variously under the rather grandiose titles of The Brooklands Garage, Edmunds, Wadden & Co Ltd or Autotrix Works, but actually located in a series of lock-up stables (which still exist) at The Quadrant, Weybridge.

Edmunds was previously manager

of a cycle shop run by Mr Lavermore in Weybridge, and that business has survived to this day in the hands of Lavermore's grandson, R Lewis, well-known as one of the foremost suppliers of spares for BSA motorcycles.

Initially, Edmunds' business consisted of a cycle and motorcycle shop - The Motor Cycle Exchange - next to Mowats the fishmongers in the parade of shops behind which the stable yard was located, and this business commenced in 1911. Finance was largely provided by George Wadden, a local hairdresser who ran

Entire staff of Zenith Motors Ltd, Weybridge, *circa* 1912/13. Bob Dicker worked for the Competition Department before the Great War and his experience gained there on the Zenith 'Gradua' gear, for which Zenith machines were famous, stood him in good stead when advising Vickers on the design of a tail-raising gear for the SE5 aeroplane during the war.

Autotrix chassis awaiting bodywork [to be built by Ted Elliott] in the mews at The Quadrant, Weybridge. The cars were built in the building with the open door - The Brooklands Garage - which still houses small workshops to this day.

Early water-cooled Autotrix with rear-mounted radiator. Note the large 'A' cut into the air intake at the front of the bonnet. The young lad standing at the rear of the car is Poulter, Bob Dicker's assistant. Their fathers were both friendly, and the original photograph was signed by Poulter and given to Bob.

his salon independently of the motor business until 1939, and who became a partner.

As well as racing cycles, the tiny company also embarked upon the manufacture of the Autotrix cyclecar, so named because it was a three wheeler, and as early as April 1911, examples were being raced at Brooklands.

At the 1911 Motorcycle Show, the Autotrix was the lowest powered 'duocar' on view and, at 60 guineas, probably one of the cheapest too. Powered by a 3½hp single cylinder JAP engine mounted between the front wheels, the drive was taken by belt to a countershaft mounted on a swivelling pivot. A double pulley fitted with a sliding centre flange was attached to the countershaft, one pulley receiving the belt from the engine and the other transmitting the power through another belt to the rear wheel.

The modus operandi is worthy of mention, relying upon an infinitely variable gearing arrangement patented as the 'Auto Gradual' gear. When the gearing was raised - presumably by opening the throttle, the groove of the double pulley that took the engine drive opened, causing the other groove to close. Consequently, the belt line from the engine was slack and the other tight, and in exactly the same proportion. To remedy this, the whole countershaft was swivelled backwards. This somewhat complicated arrangement provided infinitely variable ratios between 12-1 and 3-1.

Bodywork consisted of a large wicker basket, similar to a motorcycle sidecar of the period, but the contraption boasted wheel steering and a 'free' engine - an engine, that is, which

The entire staff of the Autotrix works *circa* 1913. George Wadden is at the wheel and S Edmunds is sitting next to him wearing the trilby hat. Autotrix cars appeared in a variety of guises and this one has a frontal radiator of rather Rolls-Royce lines.

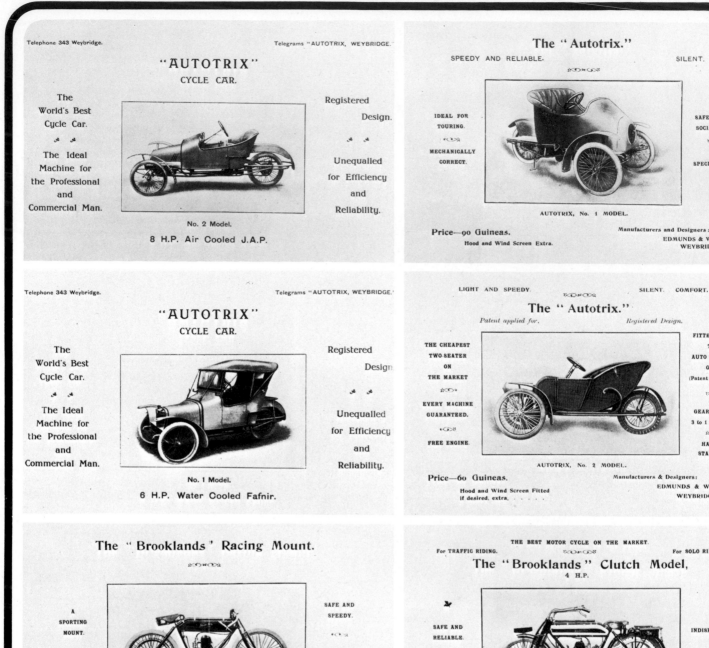

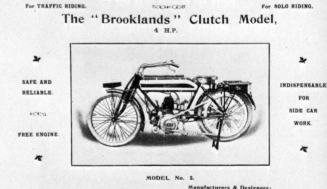

These illustrations taken from an original Autotrix catalogue illustrate the variety of models which were available, one even with a wickerwork body! The two models of The Brooklands motorcycle are also interesting since the make is not recorded in Tragatsch or other normal reference sources.

could be started at rest, with the gears being engaged via a clutch, and which was not, therefore, necessary to stall every time the vehicle was brought to a halt.

Designated the No 2 model, this Autotrix was supplemented by a rather more substantially bodied two seater with the same mechanical specification, and by a larger 8hp type with 8/9hp JAP air-cooled vee-twin engine and Chater-Lea gearbox with final drive by chains. This latter model sported a windscreen, canvas hood and lamp set and was also available with 6hp water-cooled Fafnir engine.

In all, some thirty Autotrix cyclecars were built, none bearing much resemblance to one another except that all were three wheelers. The earlier types had rounded radiators - some with a large 'A' mounted at the front, but the later types (which were all water-cooled) sported a small squared-off design rather like a miniature Rolls-Royce.

In a letter to the journal *Motor Cycling* in April 1912, George Wadden defends the stability of his cars - and of the three wheeler in general - pointing out that the Autotrix was underslung, with a separate cradle for the rear wheel, giving a much lower centre of gravity. This correspondence followed the abandonment of the cycle car race at Brooklands on Easter Monday 1912 due to lack of entries (which George Morgan of Morgan three wheeler fame took to mean lack of sportsmanship because of the successes already clocked up by his cars) and Wadden, whilst aplauding Morgan's outburst as perhaps stirring up all supporters of cyclecars, indicated that the Autotrix would be willing to take on the Morgan at any time 'for a sporting run'.

1914 Simplic cyclecar outside Wadden & West's garage at Cobham. Power was provided by an 8hp JAP air-cooled vee twin, with long exposed belt drive passing through the rear mudguard.

As if to prove his point, an Autotrix won the BMCRC Meeting cyclecar race that month, defeating Harry Martin in a Morgan, but in fairness it must be said that Martin clearly had the fastest vehicle in the race. Unfortunately, he was handicapped out of the first three places by being sent off 'from scratch' and could manage no better than fourth place.

Bob Dicker recalls another race in which the Autotrix was leading the field, but which then broke down. So

as not to disgrace it, however, Bob pulled out one of the plug leads, and when, sometime later, the car pottered over the finishing line on only one cylinder, he was able to explain the car's poor performance was due to 'a faulty plug lead' rather than admit that anything was seriously wrong!

Not all the cars were of sporting type, however, at least four being purchased by McVities for their travellers and another two being delivered to a tea company in Hull, and another interesting sideline was the production of motorcycles. Two models were offered - a tuned version with 'fixed' engine, belt drive and single speed, specially built for racing

and with dropped handlebars, *sans* mudguards and lightweight frame - and a touring model with 'free' engine, clutch and full road-going equipment. Both appear to have been powered by JAP single cylinder side valve engines, both were belt driven and the touring model was said to be 'indispensable for side-car work', so the engine must have been of reasonable size. Alas, very little detail has survived of 'the best motorcycle on the market' and Erwin Tragatsch ignores them in both his books. They were marketed under the trade name of The Brooklands - do any survive, I wonder?

The Autotrix concern was, however, very small, supporting a staff of only ten in addition to Edmunds and Wadden and with the outbreak of war in 1914 there were more important things to do. In any event, Edmunds left the partnership in 1913 and emigrated to Sydney, Australia, the partnership broke up and, after a short spell with ABC at Hersham, Bob Dicker moved to Zenith as a tester and by the beginning of hostilities had joined Vickers.

Here, his experience with the Zenith 'Gradua' gear stood him in good stead since he was able to advise Vickers on the design of a tail raising gear for the SE5 aeroplane, which worked on the same principle. Before hostilities ceased, he had completed 1005 of these.

Whilst at Zenith, part of his duties had included 'lapping in' new bikes at Brooklands, and during this period he became friendly with a Manchester lad named Jack Alcock who was working for Du Cros (one of the earliest champions of Brooklands) and who also liked motorcycles. The two youngsters both used to ride machines at Brooklands and became firm friends.

Alcock joined the Flying Corps, became a pilot and for a time was a prisoner in Turkey - Bob recalls that the Turks used to throw stones at aircraft - and having survived this ordeal and the war itself joined Vickers as a test pilot.

The flight which he made with Lt Arthur Whitten Brown in a Vickers Vimy from Newfoundland to Ireland, arriving on 14th June 1919 in an Irish marsh earned him and Brown a place in history, and a knighthood, but his new-found fame did not spoil his friendship with Bob, who had also been a member of the Vimy team.

Jack had had his fill of flying, and largely, perhaps, because of his experience with his own 10hp Humber, he decided to set up in business with Bob Dicker as a motor agent. Humbers had apparently already approached him with the offer of an agency for their cars.

On the eve of his last flight, he said to Bob, 'I'm chucking up flying for this company, but we'll have a weekend in Paris and that'll be the

The 1914 Simplic with West and Wadden aboard showing the simplicity of construction so typical of the wire and bobbin brigade of the period. The PA series number denotes a *circa* late 1914 Surrey registration. The 'S' cut-out is reminiscent of the 'A' of the Autotrix.

end of it'. All would have been well, but on 18th December 1919, Bob received a telephone call from Maxwell Muller, the Vickers works manager, to say that Jack had crashed in fog just outside Paris and had been killed.

Tragedy seemed to dog both the transatlantic heroes - Brown married a clergyman's daughter, and they had one son. The wife later died, the son was killed in the Second World War

and Brown later committed suicide. As for Bob, he opened a cycle shop at Addleston selling most makes, including Hercules, BSA, Sun and Sunbeam but maintained his interest in motorcycling. At one stage, 'Pa' Norton asked him to ride for the Norton team in America, and Bill Wells, head of the Indian motorcycle company's English branch was also a close friend.

Meanwhile, the irrepressible Wadden had tried again. Following Edmund's departure to Australia, he formed another partnership with a man named West, and as Wadden & West took further premises at Cobham in 1914, there to design yet another cyclecar.

This time it was called The Simplic and differed substantially from the Autotrix in design and layout. In the first place it was a four wheeler and although of low build, was not underslung. Power was provided by air-cooled JAP engines of either 5/6hp or 8hp, mounted longitudinally at the front under a rounded bonnet, at the front of which was displayed a large cut-out 'S' reminiscent of the 'A' of the Autotrix.

Drive was transmitted by a long exposed belt from a countershaft just aft of the front wheels direct to the rear wheels, an epicyclic gearing was employed and the whole device was offered in 1915, despite the war, at £75. It is difficult to say how many Simplics were built, since photographs of only three - built in 1914, 1915 and 1923 - have survived.

Obviously, very few would have been built during the war and by 1919 Wadden's partnership with West had been dissolved and he was once again back in Weybridge on his own and operating from works in Jessamy Road. The post-war model differed considerably, employing a wooden chassis with quarter elliptic springing all round fitted with coil spring

Revised 1915 Simplic offered at £75. The running boards have been dispensed with, the rear of the bodywork revised with staggered seating, mudguards on the rear wheels have been re-sited to obviate cutting a hole for the belt to pass through, the forward end of the belt is shielded and additional louvres to assist cooling are cut in the bonnet.

dampers. Power was provided by a large 8-10hp JAP air-cooled vee twin via a tortuous system of chains through two countershafts to the nearside rear wheel, twin speeds being provided by what appears to have been a system of chains and sliding dogs similar to the Frazer Nash but located at the front of the car. The 1923 car was most certainly completed, since a 1924 photograph illustrates it out on a picnic, but it is doubtful if such a primitive device would have attracted many customers a year after the Austin Seven had been introduced.

Doubtless Mr Wadden found his hairdressing business more profitable and concentrated upon it thereafter, but at least he had the satisfaction of having beaten a Morgan at Brooklands, and the Autotrix did warrant a mention in the Autocar Imperial Year Book for 1914.

At 85, and retired, Bob Dicker could still recall the days when Brooklands aerodrome was the mecca for wealthy amateurs, some of them more gifted than others. Serge de Bollotoff, for example, a Russian aristocraft, who built an enormous tri-plane in one of the Brooklands sheds, and then had to dig two parallel trenches to get it out when the time came for flight tests. It never flew, of course, and hardly surprising when one learns that the redoubtable De Bollotoff sawed the ends of the propellers off to keep the revs up! Another hopeful was Bellamy, who kept a tame kestrel. He was constantly agitating the creature so that it would flap its wings. He would observe these movements carefully and then rush back to the drawing board to get it all down on paper before the image faded!

Now Bob Dicker, Edmunds, Wadden, the Autotrix, Zenith, Brooklands and Simplic machines, De Bollotoff and Bellamy have all gone, and one cannot help feeling that the world is the poorer for it.

WHENCE THE MASCOTS

**The collection of automobilia and motoring ephemera
is one of the fastest growing hobbies associated with the vintage vehicle movement,
and as complete vehicles become further and further out of reach
for those with modest pockets, has now been accepted as a convenient,
and much less expensive alternative.
Not unnaturally, one of the most popular areas concerns the collection
of radiator mascots - the sculpture of the motorcar -
and none are better qualified than DENISE FROSTICK to write about them.
Here she gives us a nostalgic glimpse of some of the designs
marketed under the Desmo trademark and reminds us that,
although one of the earliest successful firms in the business
they are still producing attractive designs today.**

'NO mascot shall be carried by a vehicle registered on or after 1st October 1937, in any position where it is likely to strike any person in a collision, if the mascot is liable to be the cause of injury by reason of any projection.'

Thus the death sentence was passed. The agony did not last long; the war came and, with it, the reign of utility. Manufacture of the mascot, a luxury article, was banned altogether, and foundries joined the war effort. Cars went into cold storage; metal was scarce; mascots, together with sauce-pans and other household articles sacrificed by patriotic housewives, went back to the foundry - this time to be melted down and recast into

The Eagle, the earliest design used as a mascot in the US was very popular in England. This is one of the largest mascots and the globe, designed to give solidity, was particularly well used by Seymour to give a downswoop of the tail and enhance the wingspan.

weapons far more lethal than mere projecting ornaments. There were, however, those who hung on to their metallic assets and, during the last twenty years, attics, cellars and that forgotten shelf at the top of the cupboard have yielded many a treasure coveted by an ever-increasing number of collectors.

It was at the turn of the century that mascots really appeared *en masse* and, in the span of forty years, a highly specialised craft was born,

The swift, registered design no 777650, is more frequently found as a later casting bearing the Desmo copyright mark. It shows quite clearly how well Seymour adapted to fashion trends.

flourished and disappeared. The men who made these mascots were never trained under a government scheme; when their jobs vanished, by government decree, they received no redundancy payment. Who were they? We know the distributors; we have the names of some of the designers; but what of the manufacturers? Desmo, for instance, whose mark appears on so many interesting specimens.

Desmo never manufactured a single mascot; they did not register any design in their own name at the Patent Office, but with their small showcase of accessories prominent in every garage, they made it possible for the small man, willing to let them put *their* name on *his* product, to survive. Competition was at its keenest in this

Another favourite from the US was Aronson's Diving Girl; reproduced by every English manufacturer it sold under the name of the Speed Nymph. Seymour's diving girls, however, owe very little to Aronson's design.

new opening, which promised to be lucrative, if not for butchers and bakers, then at least for candlestick makers. Every brass foundry in Birmingham - and indeed everywhere else - who was then turning out chandeliers, fender and hearth furniture, bedsteads, door knockers and the like, tried his hand at mascots; even the Sheffield men moved in in the 1920s.

On the Continent things were a little different and the mascot maker tended to be more in the line of the *bronzeur*; this is how Lejeune came to be the best known manufacturer in this country. The Lejeunes came from Paris in 1904 and were soon connected with the masters of this craft, not only

England has produced more animal mascots than any other country. These are three fine examples, a ram, a lion, and a terrier which could just as well grace the mantelshelf. The lion is very similar to the 1925 World Exhibition model.

in the French capital, but in Spain, Czechoslovakia, Hungary and the banks of the Danube where the industry was thriving in 4000 BC, according to Colin Renfrew, Sc D, in his fascinating article published in the *Geographical Magazine* of November 1977.

Lejeune were very soon to capture the top end of the market, whilst our Birmingham founders worked in brass to which a bronze finish was applied if desired and, later, plating in nickel, chromium, silver and, very occasionally, gold. They registered their designs with the Patent Office and this gave them protection of copyright of a registered design for a period of five years, which they could extend, once or twice, for another five years each time.

It is all too easy, however, to draw inspiration for a new design from someone else's best seller, or even to alter a best seller very slightly without infringing the copyright. A court action is lengthy and expensive, so the owner of a design seldom took the trouble to seek extended protection. The newcomer, therefore, had at his disposal, for free, the entire stock of expired copyright designs, and it is no wonder that an identical mascot should have been turned out, at the same time, in every foundry.

With the superstitious, the horseshoe was always a favourite.

Many a well-to-do motorist had a collection of mascots suitable for the occasion and used to choose from them as carefully as he would select the appropriate club tie. There were mascots for going to the races, to the greyhounds, for salmon fishing expeditions and, of course, for golf. This golf ball is a Seymour registered design no 791777. Later castings bear the Desmo copyright mark.

With the twenty years' protection given in France to the *modèle déposé*, the *bronzeurs* could go to the best sculptors for their models and they seldom failed to put their foundry mark on their product. It was a very different situation.

Some time between 1900 and 1905, in Sherlock Street, Birmingham, a small brass foundry opened to turn out bedsteads, fenders and candlesticks of its own design. George E Seymour later moved to Lower Trinity Street before settling at their present address on Cheapside. They also made precision tools, which did not involve engineering, and which they designed themselves, such as a dog's tooth extractor for vets and, when war broke

While this Manikin was a special order for Belgium, a tiny mascot faithfully reproducing the little statue in Brussels.

out, they registered for the first time four patriotic mascot designs on 13th November 1914; these sold well and they are still making mascots today.

This very small firm which was formed into a limited company in 1935 made good use of the talents of George E Seymour's three sons: Eric, the designer; Stanley, the craftsman who did the sand casting; and Leslie George, the businessman who turned what had been an expensive hobby into a profitable concern. The foundry was a sideline, employing but a few men; the Seymours ran a garage, food stores, even a caravan and camping site. They did not use common brass, but fine brass which a strong hand can bend, thus giving each mascot a personal touch. They tried bronze once, for a Guy's head, and gave it up; they found it too porous.

Their mascots, beautifully chased and hand finished, were initially in polished brass to which they added other finishes with the years: oxidised bronze, silver, nickel, chromium, sending each article away for plating.

For specific cars they made the Rover Viking and a jaguar and for the manufacturer a Guy Indian plain or enamelled.

kept the entire collection, and many others not of his own firm's making, on a shelf which ran above the picture rail all round his hall - nearly one hundred of them. He died some two years ago. They buried him three days later. His son Scott S Seymour, the present owner of the firm, called at the house on the day of his death to collect some documents and did not go back there until after the funeral. Meanwhile, others had moved in: the French windows were broken, the shelf was bare .....

The thieves obviously knew what they were doing. To break up the collection would not be a profitable operation. To dispose of it openly would arouse considerable notice. Has an unsuspicious collector already acquired it? We may well wonder. Meanwhile, the firm will still make special orders at very reasonable prices and, of course, you would then have the genuine article, not a replica, not a reproduction, not a fake, but the authentic object, made from the authentic patterns, finished to the firm's traditional standards, and you would not have to ask the unanswerable question:

'Whence this mascot?'

They did one very special order for Lady Docker in gold finish but they never sold through the 'posh' firms like Dunhill. The bulk of their production went to Desmo, whose trade mark it bore, indeed still bears today.

They made the Alvis Hare, before the contract went to Lejeunes, who cast it in bronze; Desmo's Jaguar; the Guy's Indian, fully enamelled (today you have to send work of this kind away to Austria); the Sabre aircraft; a 'Sabre Jet' mounted on a Sabre for the Canadian Air Force, presented to pilots passing out at the end of their training; Sir Walter Raleigh for Raleigh cycles; Earl Haig; Charlie Chaplin; Mickey and Minnie Mouse; the Pegasus supplied to Mobil for competitors in the Mobil Economy Run; 'Sir Kreemy Nut' for Sharp's toffee, and many others ... an impressive collection, to which must be added every Girl Guide pole end.

Leslie George, to whose business acumen much of the success of the firm was due, loved these mascots. He

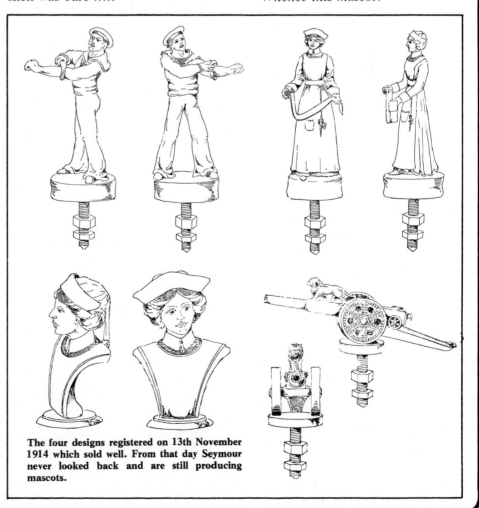

The four designs registered on 13th November 1914 which sold well. From that day Seymour never looked back and are still producing mascots.

WHITE KNIGHTS AND SILVER SLIPPERS
THE CARS OF CECIL BRINTON

In the days before and just after the First World War, it was not uncommon
for men of great wealth and with an amateur interest in automobile engineering
to construct motor cars for their personal use and to their own designs.
Best remembered of these are the Chitty-Chitty-Bang-Bang aero engined monsters
fielded by Count Louis Zborowski and built for him by Bligh Brothers of Canterbury,
the creations of Harry Hawker and Gordon Watney and other famous specials.
Here, however, we look at two previously unpublicised examples in the design
and construction of which their sponsor played a greater than usual part.

THE casual visitor to Kidderminster
will immediately be impressed by a
skyline dominated by chimneys -
factory chimneys. The majority of
these Victorian edifices - a relic of
those 'dark and satanic mills' written
of by William Blake - are the property
of Brintons Ltd (and not a few bear
the name in lighter coloured brick) the
carpet manufacturers who are, even
today, probably the largest employers
in the area.

The company, which is still
controlled by the Brinton family,
commenced business in 1723 at Hill
Pool, a hamlet between Chaddesley
Corbett and Bellbroughton on the
outskirts of Kidderminster, and some
of the original machinery is still
preserved there.

Cecil Brinton was the seventh son of
John Brinton, MP, of Moor Hall,
Stourport-on-Severn, was born in
London on 25th April 1883 and was
educated at Cheltenham College and
Caius College, Cambridge. There he
won the Salomons' Engineering
Scholarship and took an Honours
Degree in Engineering. He was a
contemporary of Harry (later Sir

**Cecil Brinton awheel at an early age. The
tricycle is a Psycho of about 1888.**

**A motoring oddity. Cecil Brinton - in the
passenger seat - takes a ride in a *circa* 1901
Sunbeam Mabley voiturette fitted with 2¾hp
De Dion Bouton engine. Quite a few of these
found customers up until 1904.**

Cecil Brinton with one of his earliest motorised mounts. There is a hint of Rex about the machine - can anyone identify it? *Circa* 1905.

1904 10/12hp two cylinder Argyll rear entrance tonneau photographed by Cecil Brinton outside the family home.

The horizontal steam engine built by Cecil Brinton in the Cheltenham College workshops in 1899, and which powered all machinery in the Yew Tree House workshop where his Specials were built.

Harry) Ricardo, the world famous engineer and expert on internal combustion engines, whose research establishment still flourishes at Shoreham in Sussex. Both men were at Cambridge, and maintained a lively correspondence on automobile engineering matters in later life.

In 1904 he joined the family firm and was placed in charge of the engineering section and here very successfully re-designed the gripper Axminster loom first invented in 1893 by another Brinton employee, Thomas Greenwood. 1908 saw him establishing a branch factory at Peterborough, Ontario, and in 1909 he became a director of Brintons Ltd.

As one would expect, however of the winner of a scholarship set up by Sir David Salomons, Cecil Brinton took a close interest in all matters pertaining to the motor car, and as early as 1904 he designed and built himself a car. Unfortunately, no details of this early effort have survived except the registration number 0-4. An early Birmingham number, this was transferred to various family cars down the years and now graces the Bentley of Sir Tatton Brinton, MP.

In 1910, however, a second car was designed and built, and this was an altogether more ambitious project. Based on the chassis of a large Calthorpe previously owned by the family and registered 0-3755, this was rebodied with a most attractive two seater body in the shape of a lady's slipper and was promptly christened the *Silver Slipper*. Before the final shape was arrived at, the car ran with various prototype bodies, photographs of which have fortunately survived, and was licensed in East Lothian in order to secure the registration number SS 227 (the SS standing for *Silver Slipper*, of course).

By far the most unusual feature of the car, however, was the engine - a Vee Six designed and built by Brinton

Family gathering. Cecil Brinton is on the left in a large unidentified chain driven car; in the centre an 8/10hp 4 cyl Humber and on the right a 1907 Riley 9hp twin. Photo taken Saturday, 18th January 1908.

This is one of Cecil Brinton's earliest Specials with its creator at the wheel. Its basis is unknown.

The Brinton family setting out on an Edwardian picnic. Left to right: Enfield 'built like a gun', Minerva, and Wolseley 16/20 *circa* 1910. The small car at the far right is an older horizontal engined Wolseley *circa* 1904.

himself with castings made in the foundry of the Kidderminster carpet factory. Machining and bench testing were, however, completed in a fully equipped home workshop of some size which had been constructed at his home at Yew Tree House, Belbroughton. Motive power for the overhead line shafting which drove all the machines, lathes, shapers and cutters was provided by a medium sized horizontal single cylinder steam engine also built by Cecil Brinton in the workshops of Cheltenham College in 1899.

The car's engine with a bore and stroke of 2-5/8ins x 3ins, cylinders set at 90° and cranks set at 120°, was unconventional even for 1910, and an examination of the details of its construction further illustrates the innovative nature of its design. Valves - inlet and exhaust - were overhead and operated by exposed pushrods but the sparking plugs were also located in an inclined position in the cylinder heads. Two separate ignition systems catered for each bank of cylinders, the water jackets of which were fabricated from bolted-up sheet steel (rather like the later Hungarian Fejes from which Cyril Pullin derived his 10hp Ascot, except that they both employed welded-up construction of sheet steel).

Connecting rods, drilled for lightness, were 'yoked' at the 'big end' rather like the 'Scotch Yoke' principle advocated by the late S S Tresilian and employed in the American K-D (Knight-Davidson) split sleeve valve engine designed by Margaret Knight (no relation to Charles Yale Knight) for her cars in 1913.

Despite such unorthodoxy, however, the engine ran successfully for more than 10,000 miles before being replaced by a re-designed Model T Ford unit and such was the affection which the car engendered that a close friend was moved to dedicate the following poem to it in March 1912:-

Speed, Silver Slipper, speed,
Under your flying wheels the white
road burns.
Swing down the slopes; of gradient
take no heed.
Speed, Silver Slipper, speed.

Through windswept space, past
moor, and copse, and mead,
While dawn to noon, and noon to
darkness turns,
Speed, Silver Slipper, speed,
Under your flying wheels, the white
road burns.
K.C.B.

Cecil Brinton looking justly proud of his 1911 creation, *The Silver Slipper.* **Apart from the lightened axle, it bears little resemblance to the former Calthorpe.**

The V6 dismantled to show its unusual features. It ran for some 10,000 miles with varying success.

Cecil Brinton was in charge of the famous carpet firm's engineering department and as a result had access to the foundry in which were cast the crankcase and gearbox housing for *The Silver Slipper* **in 1910.**

Of course, its behaviour was not always quite so exemplary - in April 1912, the same *K.C.B.* was writing to Cecil, 'The *Silver Slipper* must pull herself together and behave like a lady without any further delay .....', but nevertheless it seems to have performed well enough generally. The writer was fortunate in discovering most of the parts of the engine scattered around in outhouses at Yew Tree House some four years ago, together with most of the wooden patterns used to cast the aluminium crankcase and gearbox housing, and these are now preserved by Mike Cummins of the Alvis Owners Club. After 10,000 miles the surviving connecting rods are showing signs of breaking up - particularly where drilled - but nevertheless it must be said that Cecil Brinton must have been an extremely gifted amateur designer.

He was, of course, not without experience of motor cars, having owned a succession of motorcycles and cars - including a 6hp 2 cylinder 1901 Star, a 10/12hp 2 cylinder Argyll of 1904 manufacture and various other 'specials' with belt and chain drive.

The search for perfection continued, however, and in 1919 a further project was commenced. The body of the *Silver Slipper* was appropriated for this and was itself replaced by a more modern four seater tourer of rather square lines, allied to a radiator of rather Rolls-Royce appearance.

The new car, which inherited the *Slipper* body, appears to have been based on a small Daimler or BSA

Cecil Brinton at the wheel of the re-bodied *Silver Slipper* in July 1913. This body was subsequently used on the White Knight in 1919.

In 1907 Cecil Brinton had visited Canada and brought back this photograph of a Grand Rapids, Michigan-built Austin. Known as The Highway King, the make foundered in 1921 and is not to be confused with the Austin of his native Midlands.

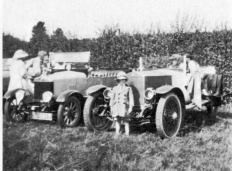

Out on the open road with *Silver Slipper* and friends. At the rear is an EMF, then *The Slipper* with *circa* 1912 10/12hp Belsize and what appears to be an 8/10hp Marlborough [or could it be a Wilton?] in front.

Another Brinton Special, believed to be a Birmingham-built Turner-based Universal of around 1914.

chassis - certainly it is fitted with a Knight-type double sleeve valve engine, numbered 18998 and manufactured by Daimler under licence from Knight & Kilbourne Patents Ltd (the company set up by Charles Yale Knight in order to collect his patent royalties).

Drive is taken through a large three speed gearbox of unknown make to an overhead worm rear axle which would not appear to be of Daimler origins. The engine number dates it at *circa* 1913, so it was probably a secondhand unit when purchased and the records which have survived do not indicate that the family owned either a small Daimler or BSA.

This car, which was originally painted white (including the radiator), with black wings, white rubber tyres and sporting a silver knight chessman on the radiator cap, was christened the *White Knight* in deference to its engine's designer, and has happily survived. It was discovered about four years ago in an open shed on the Yew Tree House estate and is now being restored by Mike Cummins. Everything was complete except for the throttle quadrant on the steering column and the headlights. By a stroke of pure luck, the latter were spotted mounted on poles at either end of what had once been elegant tennis courts, but which had been ploughed up in the wartime 'Dig for Victory' campaign. Evidently, and Cecil Brinton is known to have been a keen sportsman, house parties at the

An unlikely car for a millionaire to own! Cecil Brinton in characteristic pose with the Model T Ford. The engine from this car was later installed, after modification, in *The Silver Slipper* to replace the V6.

The Silver Slipper in its final form with Rolls-Royce style radiator. Note the drilled front axle which can be traced back to the Calthorpe. The car was scrapped in the twenties though its final body has survived. On the left is a Standard.

The designer/manufacturer at the wheel of the newly completed White Knight, April 1919.

The White Knight ready for road test early in 1919. Though it acquired *The Silver Slipper's* body, it was mechanically related to the sleeve valve BSA/Daimler.

Cecil Brinton inspecting a racing Sunbeam nicknamed *Raffles* - probably at Shelsley in 1921.

Cecil Brinton always had a soft spot for the locally made Calthorpes and he photographed this racer in 1921 being weighed, probably at Shelsley Walsh.

A roadside picnic in the late twenties. The leading car is a Rover - probably a 16/50 of about 1928. The headlights mounted on the radiator shell were a Rover feature of the period. The car in the background is the Brinton 'Twenty' Rolls.

Brinton family line-up at Yew Tree House in the thirties. Gone are the Specials and in their place are, left to right: a brace of Wolseley Hornets for son and daughter, Riley Kestrel, Rolls Twenty with CJB, and on the far right a *Silver Ghost* in the care of the chauffeur.

A '27 Cowley with Cecil's wife Cathleen in the dickey seat. They were married in 1912 and she died in 1954, he in 1970.

A Brinton family wedding. The leading car is a Sunbeam whilst a more humble Cowley brings up the rear.

All that remains intact of Cecil Brinton's motoring creations - the White Knight in 1974 with Mr Fox head gardener at Yew Tree House before the car was taken away to be restored.

Brinton home involved floodlit games on the courts in the evenings!

The *White Knight* inherited 0-4 from one of its predecessors, but is now wearing SS 227 since the *Silver Slipper* now has a separate existence only in certain engine and body parts - although the last body with which it was fitted has also survived.

Cecil Brinton was, in fact, a man of many parts. In his youth a Cambridge 'blue', he rowed in his college 'first' boat and at Henley Regatta - in which event his crew won the Thames Cup in 1904. As passionately interested in aviation as he was in motoring and engineering generally, he built a powered model before the turn of the century, took a keen interest in all the new aeroplane designs and attended the Schneider Trophy races.

An animal lover, he was particularly fond of his dogs, all of which were embalmed and placed in proper coffins upon their deaths. He had designed, and always intended to build in the grounds of Yew Tree House, a miniature mausoleum in which to house the remains of these faithful friends, but at his death at the age of 87 in 1970 this wish remained unfulfilled.

A musician, he had installed at the great hall at Yew Tree House an enormous four-bank organ of cathedral proportions, he built a puppet theatre in the garden - The Hetherington Theatre Royal - enjoyed amateur dramatics, was a councillor, politician, High Sheriff and Mayor, and devoted some 65 years to the service of the company he helped so greatly to expand.

From our point of view, however, it is perhaps fortunate that his divers interests also embraced photography. From an early date he meticulously recorded every minute event in the life of the family, developing and printing the results in his own studio, and a large number of finished prints and glass plate negatives were found following his death. Just a fraction of them are reproduced here - glimpses of Edwardian life in the grand manner preserved in aspic - a unique record of both the cars (and the models, for he exhibited regularly at the Model Engineers Exhibition in the twenties) and the man. We would have liked to have known him.

Reviews

The lot of the specialist book reviewer is a mixed one, and like the curate's egg, parts of it are excellent. Since motoring history became respectable, it seems that every publisher in the business finds at least one motoring title a year mandatory, but the number who take the subject seriously are, sadly, still few and far between. Whilst, obviously, no single book list can be definitive, and a great deal depends on individual taste, the value of a good library to both enthusiast and historian alike is inestimable. *VINTAGE CAR ANNUAL* will, therefore, be reviewing selected books but only those which we feel merit inclusion and recommendation. Obviously, not all books which are available can be included in these pages, and lack of mention does not automatically mean an indictment. We will, however, endeavour to include a representative selection of the best.

THE MOTOR CAR 1946-1956 by Michael Sedgwick. [B T Batsford. £15.00. Hardback.] With the exception of David Culshaw's admirable *The Motor Guide to Makes and Models*, first published twenty years ago, very little has been written on the *general* post-war scene. Whilst it may be a difficult pill to swallow for those who, like this reviewer, commenced their motoring during the mid-fifties, the fact is that cars of the forties and fifties are now history, and never before has there been so much interest in them.

Michael Sedgwick needs no introduction to most enthusiasts, and as author of *Cars of the Thirties* from the same publishers, is eminently qualified to write its sequel. Arguably the best of the current school of motoring historians, he is no newcomer and his writings over the past twenty years or so have been authoritative, entertaining and prodigious. Not only this, but he is multi-lingual and this enables him to correspond with enthusiasts worldwide on a level denied to most others. The result is that, whether writing about the cars of Germany or France, Japan or Russia or of his own native Britain, he manages to grasp not only the essential technical and historical details of the vehicles but the very essence and background of the country in which they were built and the mentality of those who built them.

It might be thought that the period chosen is an odd one - indeed, the author commences his *Introduction* with an apologia, although proceeding to justify it admirably. No such justification is necessary, in the opinion of this reviewer. The fifties were, as Rene Cutforth has said, 'the watershed decade of the century'. It was the decade in which the very old met the very new, a decade of sharp contrasts - of ballroom dancing and rock'n roll when it came to music, cars, manners and mores.

The period is divided into three distinct phases in the development of the post-war car - initially, the continuation of 1939-40 formulae followed by the emergence of the 'new line' and the true post-war car with, finally, designs which were totally divorced from the pre-1940 concept. Taking each country in turn, and covering not only the major manufacturing nations like the United States, Britain, Germany, France and Italy, but also Spain, Belgium, Holland, Austria, Switzerland, Czechoslovakia, Russia, Australia and Japan and even including Poland, Denmark, Norway, Sweden and Argentina, the book explores via an introductory essay in each case the general manufacturing background. There then follows

an in-depth study of every significant sector of the market, and as in previous books, the scope of these chapters can be judged from Michael's amusing chapter titles. For example, his treatment of the mini-car boom in the British section of the book comes under the heading of *Super Scooters for Suez*, and although we tried, we couldn't catch him out and there appeared to be no bubble car or other mini-horror omitted.

Similarly, the introductory essay on Japan was entitled *Will the Sun Never Rise*, and certainly few could have divined that from such unpromising beginnings, Japan would have risen to the position of supremacy she enjoys in the world of motor manufacture today. From the Datsun to the ephemeral Suminoe Flying Feather, all are faithfully documented - not as a tedious buyer's guide of names and specifications, but with interesting information like performance, production figures, prices and general marketing background to give proper perspective in each case.

It would be difficult to pinpoint any area in which the same overall informative attention to detail has not been given, but quite apart from his enviable skill in prising loose hitherto unknown facts and setting them down in readable fashion, is Michael Sedgwick's talent for analysing what he has written and coming up with the kind of conclusions which are so logical that the reader forgets that they were not previously obvious and says to himself, 'Why didn't I think of that?'

Michael has his own very personal style of writing, and if I have any criticisms at all it is in those instances where over-zealous proof readers decide to re-write his prose. Thus '.... had given it best' becomes ' ....had given their best' - not the same thing at all, but *I* know the way Michael intended it, even if his publishers do not. There are other annoying little items like this, but 99% of readers will miss them unless they, too, receive frequent letters from the author and know the way his mind works.

There is so much information in the book, and it gives such a good coverage of the era, that it is as valuable as a social and economic history of the period as it is to the car enthusiast. Michael knows his cars. He *likes* the thirties, forties and fifties, which is perhaps half the battle, and illustrates graphically that, far from being dull, the period was absolutely bursting with innovation and development, albeit much of it misguided and/or stillborn.

I confidently predict that *The Motor Car 1946-1956* will become the standard work on the period and it was, therefore, a little disappointing that Batsford apparently have so little faith in its hardback mass sales that they have stuck a price of £15 on it. This will inhibit it, doubtless, but if - as I hope they will - the publishers are not tardy in bringing out the paperback edition, then the book will undoubtedly find the wide audience it richly deserves.

BY JUPITER! The Life of Sir Roy Fedden by Bill Gunston. [Royal Aeronautical Society, London. £5.00.] In 1975 this reviewer was engaged in research for a book published by the Institute of Mechanical Engineers and written with L J K Setright, entitled *Some Unusual Engines*. Three facts emerged as a result of this research and stood out among all the rest. The first was that warfare advances technology, the second that no study of the internal combustion engine can be conducted without encompassing all its applications on land, sea or air, and the third was that two names recurred again and again. Those two names were Sir Harry Ricardo FRS and Sir Roy Fedden, and the overwhelming impression gained was of the enormous stature of these two men in their chosen fields and the importance of their respective contributions in the development of the internal combustion engine.

Sir Harry was the older of the two men, but was fortunately able to complete his autobiography first, in 1968. Roy Fedden always adopted a pretty gruff 'history is bunk' stance (like Henry Ford) on those occasions when I approached him in his Welsh retreat and mentioned the subject of an autobiography. Fortunately for us all, Bill Gunston had better luck although he admits that his relationship

with Fedden was, at best, robust and for a period amicably discontinued.

Bill Gunston requires no introduction to aviation enthusiasts - a flying instructor with the RAF before taking up writing, he was at one time technical editor of *Flight* and has many first class aviation titles to his credit. Whilst his contribution to motoring history with this book is important, therefore, it is in the world of aviation that Roy Fedden is best remembered and this explains the involvement of the Royal Aeronautical Society.

But there is plenty of motoring content, too. From Fedden's early association with Straker-Squire and Shamrock cars, his Brooklands exploits, the Cosmos organisation which was responsible for the Cosmos and CAR radial air-cooled people's car to his significant involvement with the Burt McCollum single sleeve valve engine. Where Argyll failed, Fedden succeeded and the re-purchase of the patents from Continental of America heralded a whole new line of successful aero engines just when Britain needed them. Aircraft such as the *Tempest*, the *Fury* and the *Typhoon* (the *Fury* at well over 480 mph at 20,000 feet) used single sleeve valve engines to good effect during and after World War II.

After the war Fedden designed a rear engined, three cylinder water-cooled radial engine with vertical crankshaft and this was fitted to a number of prototypes which echoed some of Preston Tucker's thinking in America. This saga is documented as is the personality of the man himself. Emerging as a paradoxical gentle and kind martinet, he drove his loyal staff frequently beyond endurance, but never less than he drove himself. Upbraided for being difficult to get on with, he replied, 'Nonsense, I just prefer to have my own way'.

This then is the full story of Fedden's 'way'. It is unexpurgated - which, had Fedden lived, it is unlikely to have been - and published with the blessing of his widow, Lady Norah. It chronicles faithfully the love-hate relationship which existed between Fedden and the White family who controlled Bristol Aircraft Company for so long, of his intolerance of delay of any kind and of his, at times, impossible genius.

Fedden was a Titan. As Gunston says, so powerful was his personality and so intense his way of working that even a few minutes in his presence could leave people sucked dry, like a limp rag. Yet many people who suffered this daily were glad to go on until they dropped. They knew that he was a man of destiny. He made many enemies and inspired tremendous loyalty. His relentless search for perfection led this intuitive engineer - one of the greatest - to make himself a tyrant, and at times he stretched the allegiance of even his closest friends.

This is the story of his stormy and monumental life. Of the sixty years he devoted to his work, of his triumphs and his failures, his motor cars, engines and aeroplanes. The book is only issued as a paperback, but the information it contains is well worth the money. Thank goodness it was written in time.

DEUTSCHE KLEINWAGEN by Hanns Peter Rosellen. [Bleicher Verlag Motorbuch Verlag. £13.50.] Bearing in mind that, since the 1920s, Germany has been the spiritual home of the mini-car and that, with the exception of Great Britain, no other country has influenced their design to such a degree, it is understandable and right that the first definitive work covering the fascinating period of small car development after the last war in Germany should be written in German and published in Germany.

It is only when you examine in any detail the 'bubble' car era in Britain that you realise the full extent to which German designers and manufacturers orchestrated the growth in popularity of these tiny, but often totally practical offerings - Isetta, Heinkel, Trojan and Messerschmidt, to say nothing of the infinite confections from the drawing board of Egon Brutsch, who laid his eggs as prolifically around Europe as Marcel Violet had done two decades before.

What Herr Rosellen does is to introduce us, in depth, not only to the familiar names but to the ephemerals of the post-war scene: the Meyra, the Hoffman Auto-Kabine, the Champion, Kleinschnittger (not so ephemeral with 3000 produced), and many others. In fact, we could not catch the author out and every make we had ever vaguely heard of was included. A twenty-year-old mystery was also explained for this reviewer - a peculiar little vehicle rejoicing in the name RAF, seen in Germany in 1958 whilst serving with the British organisation of the same name, turns out to be a member of the Maico/Champion family - a fact uncovered nowhere else in the intervening period.

Photographs are excellent - many of them previously unpublished fascinating views of unlikely prototypes - and both the detailed technical specifications which chronicle the development from oblivion (to, in most cases, oblivion) of a whole host of hopefuls and the potted histories which accompany them are comprehensive and a true work of scholarship. Had such a book been written about cyclecars within ten years of the demise of the last of them, historians would have a far easier task in unravelling the more obscure examples today. Would it be too much to ask the publishers to produce an English language edition?

ROLLS-ROYCE: The Growth of a Firm.
ROLLS-ROYCE: The Years of Endeavour.
ROLLS-ROYCE: The Merlin at War. By Ian Lloyd. [MacMillan. £10.00 each.] It might be thought that there was nothing left to say about Rolls-Royce but this new trilogy from the pen of Ian Lloyd does just that. As another reviewer points out, this history is purely economic, however, 'viewing Rolls-Royce as the national institution one might expect of a Conservative MP'. The interesting point is, however, that when the bulk of the trilogy was first committed to paper, Ian Lloyd was most certainly not an MP - in fact, could hardly have known that he would become one - and virtually the whole work formed the thesis for his degree at Cambridge in 1949.

That it has not been published before (except for the purposes of the degree) is largely due to the terms under which Ernest Hives (later Lord Hives) originally gave the young postgraduate permission to base his studies on the result of his unfettered access to all Rolls-Royce papers and personnel. Such is the optimism of youth that Lloyd never doubted that Hives' dictum that subsequent publication would be a matter for discussion would mean other than the formality of ratification. In fact, it was to amount to total censorship.

And in a way it's a good thing. It meant that, believing he would not be censored, Lloyd was quite fearless in his reportage. It also meant that, encouraged, he proceeded with his study of the company at a time when much in the way of documentation still survived, and many employees were still with the company who had seen it through its formative years. Had Lloyd known that Hives - in common with his tutors at Cambridge - considered the work too controversial, it is doubtful whether it would have been written at all, let alone in the form in which it now appears.

If ever a series of books took the lid off a company and shattered the hallowed shiboleths of three quarters of a century, this is it. Yes, it is heavy going at times and, given the same facilities, Graham Robson might have made a better job of it, but that (bearing in mind all the circumstances) could never have been.

What emerges is a fascinating collection of facts which could literally not have been assembled in any other way. From the initial and precarious situation which under-capitalisation brought about in 1906 to a financial crisis in the early 1920's for which Basil Johnson (Claud's brother) was made the scapegoat, from the ill-fated Springfield venture to the proposed Pierce-Arrow merger and the adoption of the D12 Curtiss aero engine in 1926 which undoubtedly kept Rolls-Royce afloat through the Depression, it is all faithfully recorded. The boardroom rows, the politics, the mistakes and the successes.

Understandably, the aero engine side of the business is well covered, but where the book is most valuable is in providing the 'inside' information, armed with which it is now possible to obtain a more balanced view of events in Rolls-Royce history, the results of which we knew but the causes of which we did not.

The trilogy takes us up to 1945 effectively, and there is, therefore, room for another volume in the history if Mr Lloyd can be persuaded to write it. If he does - and if, of course, he receives the same cooperation from the present company as an MP as he did when a student, then let us hope that we don't have to wait another thirty years to read it.

First edition copyright Marshall, Harris & Baldwin 1979.
IBSN 0 90611608 2

Published by: Published by: Marshall Harris & Baldwin Ltd.
17 Air Street
London, W.1.

Registered in London 1410311.

Designed by: Brian Harris

Printed by: Printed by: Plaistow Press Ltd., New Plaistow Road, London, E.15.

RESETTLEMENT ADVICE

MOTOR INDUSTRY JUBILEE

HUMBER·HILLMAN
SUNBEAM·TALBOT
COMMER·KARRIER

Rootes

HUMBER

PRODUCTS OF THE ROOTES GROUP